THE
BUDDHA'S BOOK
of Daily Meditations

THE
BUDDHA'S BOOK
of Daily Meditations

A Year of
Wisdom, Compassion, and
Happiness

Edited by
CHRISTOPHER TITMUSS

THREE RIVERS PRESS
NEW YORK

Published by Three Rivers Press, New York, New York.
Member of the Crown Publishing Group.

Random House, Inc. New York, Toronto, London, Sydney, Auckland
www.randomhouse.com

Three Rivers Press and the Tugboat design are registered trademarks of Random House, Inc.
Originally published in Great Britain by Rider, an imprint of Ebury Press, Random House, in 2001.

Printed in the United States of America

DESIGN BY KAREN MINSTER

Library of Congress Cataloging-in-Publication Data

The Buddha's book of daily meditations : a year of wisdom, compassion, and happiness / edited by Christopher Titmuss.
    Includes index.
    1. Buddhist devotional calendars.   2. Buddhist meditations.
I. Titmuss, Christopher.
  BQ5579 .B83   2001
  294.3'4432—dc21

                                                            2001037036

ISBN 0-609-80780-3

10 9 8 7 6 5 4 3 2 1

First American Edition

CONTENTS

INTRODUCTION

I was delighted when Judith Kendra, Publishing Director of Rider Books at Random House UK, invited me to select 365 pieces for *The Buddha's Book of Daily Meditations*. It is a wonderful opportunity to express my gratitude to one of the most remarkable men who walked on this earth. Among Buddhists and non-Buddhists alike, the Buddha is still the leading voice for living with wisdom and compassion, and for realising an enlightened life.

I regard the Buddha as my teacher, friend and guide. I came across his teachings (the Dharma) in India in 1967. I don't think I've gone a day without feeling blessed at having exposure to the Buddha, the Dharma and the Sangha of men and women committed to the Dharma. During my six years as a Buddhist monk, I received Vipassana training in the Theravada tradition, the oldest of the Buddhist traditions, in Thailand. For the past 25 years, I have considered myself a servant of the Buddha through sharing the Dharma of awakening worldwide.

The beneficial influence of the Buddha falls into three primary areas.

~The First Great Benefit ~
NON-HARMING

The Buddha spoke tirelessly about engaging in a way of life that resolutely refuses to justify causing harm and suffering to others. Do we support war that generates unimaginable suffering to soldiers, civilians, animals and the environment? Do we deliberately use harsh words designed to hurt the feelings of others? With an impassioned concern, he consistently reminded humanity of our personal responsibility to look at our actions to see what causes suffering.

In a celebrated statement, he said 'I declare there is suffering in this world. I declare there is the resolution of suffering.' In many respects, people haven't changed at all. For countless centuries, everyone has met similar issues in daily life. I realised that wherever we find wisdom, we find the Buddha. The Buddha said that even if someone grabs at his clothes, they do not touch him. 'Only one who sees the Dharma sees the Buddha.'

To understand the Buddha's teachings of non-harming, we need to experience a deep intimacy with others. What the Buddha discovered applies as much today as it did when he was alive. In this intimacy with past, present and future, we experience a profound sense of non-difference. Initially, what we see in others is the interaction of body, speech and mind, just as we experience in ourselves. Nobody is fundamentally different from anybody else. If we truly understand this, we treat others as we wish them to treat us. In deep intimacy, non-harming transforms from an ethical practice into a realisation of oneness in relationship. Whenever we find the heart's expression of a non-harming way of life, we find the Buddha.

~ The Second Great Benefit ~
MEDITATION

The Buddha emphasised the importance of meditation as a vital feature in the range of his teachings. At times, it is hard to imagine how people get by in their daily lives without regular meditation to help them stay grounded in the moment. Authentic meditation examines every area of the inner life. Meditation means to sit, walk, stand, recline, with dedicated attention and clarity in the here and now. The Buddha said that meditation concerns itself with calm and insight (*samatha* and *vipassana; vi-passana* = in-seeing). In an exquisite analogy, he said calm and insight are like two birds that fly through windows of the castle. The castle means the body and the sense doors refer to the windows. The two birds bring to awareness (the lord of the castle) the message of liberation.

Through *samatha,* we discover depths of contentment, peace of mind and opening out of the contracted heart. Through insight, we see into hindrances of the mind, dissolve the power of the ego and get to know ourselves thoroughly. The Buddha makes clear the priority for calm and insight through focused inquiry into the nature of the body, feelings, states of mind and the Dharma of daily life.

The Buddha reminds us that wherever we go in the world, our mind and body go along with us. This is our instrument not only for contact with the world, but also for contact with ourselves. If there is a lack of wisdom in our inner life, we suffer and others suffer. Our brothers and sisters in the Christian tradition point out that there are sins of commission and sins of omission. Sins of commission mean the deliberate attempt to cause others suffering through acts of body, speech and mind. We easily fall prey to such patterns in order to get what we want.

Sins of omission mean that the individual does not intentionally cause suffering but brings it about for others through lack of awareness or neglect.

Empathy for the feelings of others emerges out of deep and regular meditation. We can understand the pain of others, even if it is not our personal experience. True empathy changes behaviour patterns. The Buddha points to awareness and resolution of suffering, intentional and unintentional, as much as possible. In meditation this becomes clear.

Mindfulness and awareness in daily life, along with formal meditation, contribute to a depth of *samadhi*. There is no equivalent for this word in the English language. It communicates meditative concentration, inner stability, sublime joy and true peace of mind. In *samadhi*, there is a steadfast focus. One is centred in the here and now. Not surprisingly, the Buddha placed importance on not clinging to events of past, present or future, not grasping experiences, things or situations. Through non-grasping, we experience natural *samadhi*.

~The Third Great Benefit ~
WISDOM

With regard to his teachings, the Buddha urged followers of the Dharma to use their discernment. He did not want us to agree with his every word. He spoke without fear or favour. The public image that the Buddha was holier-than-thou doesn't fit in with the Buddhist texts, known as the Pali Suttas. At times, he spoke bluntly. When he was offered a woman for pleasure, he described the body as a 'thing full of urine and excrement'. He also spoke with poetic sweetness comparing life to a 'dewdrop on the tip of a blade of grass'.

The Buddha taught a down-to-earth wisdom. He told us to shake off our obsession with the pursuit of pleasure and wake up. He showed no regard for the traditional guru-disciple relationship. He spoke as an adult to adults. He referred to himself as a 'good friend'. It was a revolutionary message calling for revolutionary change in personal, social, religious and political life. For the Buddha, four things mattered—suffering, the causes of suffering, a profound liberation and the way to realise liberation.

The Buddha indicated that right understanding means the problem stands under us and ceases to trouble our minds. To understand is to dissolve wanting and clinging. The inner suffering has then gone. Wisdom enables clear action to be taken as an outcome. In the cessation of suffering and dissatisfaction, there is the knowing of a timeless freedom we cannot measure, that death cannot take away. The Buddha said that this is Nirvana.

Just as the sun shines, whether there are clouds or not, so freedom shines through our variety of experiences. When we live a truly noble way of life, we experience this great liberation from one day to the next. It is not some absolute state to escape into, nor an occasional taste of feeling free when things are going our way.

There is nothing more worthwhile than knowing deep down an enlightened way of being. Nothing in transient existence has the power to take this enlightenment away. In this very life, we can know intimately what the Buddha understood. It is no easy undertaking to end karma conclusively, namely the painful influences upon our inner lives of the past on the present. It is no easy task to explore what it means to lead an utterly fulfilled life without becoming spellbound by religious and scientific beliefs. To step out of the imprisonment of unhealthy and unsatisfactory states of mind marks the standpoint of liberation.

What is enlightenment? It is an umbrella concept referring to knowing a profoundly liberating wisdom. This includes realisation of the Unconditioned (Nirvana, the Deathless, Liberation) that embraces past, present and future. An enlightened one understands the conditions for suffering and the resolution of them. He or she respects and applies the ethics of non-harming, meditation and wisdom.

Deep friendship for all beings fills the heart of the enlightened ones. There is the capacity to stay steady in the midst of pressure, to abide fearlessly in difficult circumstances. Enlightened ones experience absence or virtual absence of problems in their daily lives and much happiness in the ordinary. They reveal a wonderful generosity of spirit.

I believe in the historical person of the Buddha for one reason. The texts show a depth of experience and understanding which in my view would be inaccessible to a thinker, academic or philosopher. The Dharma, that is the teachings and practices to realise an enlightened life, clearly emerges out of profound experiences and insights, not just the result of a clever mind.

My deepest gratitude goes to the Buddhas of past, present and future for pointing out the unsurpassable Dharma that enlightens the lives of humanity.

CHRISTOPHER TITMUSS

A NOTE TO THE READER

I wish to express my immense gratitude to the tradition of Buddhist monk-scholars of Sri Lanka who have worked tirelessly for years to make the discourses (suttas) of the Buddha available to the English-speaking world. This book would not be possible without their noble work. Such monks, past and present, as Bhikkhu Nanatiloka, Bhikkhu Nanamoli, Bhikkhu Nanaponika, Bhikkhu Narada Thera, Bhikkhu Bodhi and the Buddhist Publication Society of Kandy, Sri Lanka, have contributed significantly to our understanding of the Dharma.

I have selected the most authoritative translations of the suttas available in the English language. I have remained very respectful to these eminent translators. I have made only modest changes, including editing the length of some sentences or making some deletions where there is repetition. It is commonly agreed that some words translated from the Pali are difficult to communicate in English in a single word. At times, English does not have the subtlety of concepts used in Pali to describe this vast field of experience. The Buddha encouraged use of contemporary language and occasionally I have done exactly that.

I have used the more common Sanskrit spelling of Dharma rather than the Pali spelling of Dhamma. At times I have made changes where appropriate. These include:

+ lust or sense desire *to* pursuit of pleasure, desire for sensual satisfaction
+ renunciation *to* giving up, letting go
+ deliverance *to* freedom
+ concentration *to* meditative concentration
+ being *to* becoming
+ holy life *to* spiritual life
+ disciples *to* students
+ dependent origination *to* dependent arising
+ right view *to* right understanding
+ Brahmins *to* priests
+ Voidness *to* Emptiness
+ Tathagata *to* One Thus Gone (beyond all wanting and clinging; name for a fully liberated one)

I believe such slight changes will help readers to understand the heart of the Buddha's teachings. His words serve as a foundation for one of the world's great religions and, more importantly, he shows humanity the way to end suffering. Readers may regard some of the Buddha's insights as obscure and difficult to comprehend. This will not be the case for everybody, and those who have explored the depths of inner experience, particularly through meditation, will understand them easily. It would water down the teachings to leave out these passages.

It is important to remember that this is a book of meditations. It is not intended as a light read. You may need to read, reflect and meditate upon some extracts from the discourses several times to get a sense of what the Buddha is pointing out. At times, the Buddha observed Noble Silence to communicate profound teachings. The meditation for April 22 consists of a blank page to indicate the inability of words to express the inexpressible.

I wish to express deepest gratitude to Wisdom Publications, the Buddhist publishers of Boston, USA, who kindly gave permission to use quotes from the Middle Length Discourses, Longer Discourses and the Connected Discourses of the Buddha. Some 60 per cent of the quotes in this book come from these three volumes.

Wisdom Publications engaged in an enormous financial undertaking to publish these three books which amount in total to some 4,000 pages of texts. They showed an extraordinary generosity of spirit to give another major publishing house permission to use some 200 quotes from three of the main texts in their catalogue. It reflects their determination to make the precise teachings of the Buddha available to as many people as possible.

Finally, I would like to thank the Pali Text Society of Oxford, England, founded in 1881, whose staff and translators have made available these sacred texts.

This book of daily meditations serves as an introduction to the full discourses. I can only encourage readers of *The Buddha's Book of Daily Meditations* to take the next step and to purchase the comprehensive teachings of the Buddha found in the Middle Length Discourses,

Longer Discourses and Connected Discourses of the Buddha. I regard these books as the three jewels of all Buddhist texts. I have written about the heart of the Buddha's teachings, such as the Four Noble Truths and the Eightfold Path, in my previous book *Light on Enlightenment*.

I hope *The Buddha's Book of Daily Meditations* will inspire you to explore further his teachings of awareness, the heart, meditation and an enlightened wisdom.

May all beings live with clarity.
May all beings understand the nature of things.
May all beings be enlightened.

A SHORT BIOGRAPHY
OF THE BUDDHA

In the year 560 BC, Siddhartha Gautama entered this world when he was born to Queen Mahamaya under a tree in a public park in Lumbini, north India. His father, King Suddhodana, the ruler of the Sakyan kingdom, gave him the name Siddhartha which means 'Wish Fulfilled'. Queen Mahamaya died seven days after the birth and Siddhartha was brought up by her sister.

At that time, Hindu society was firmly divided into castes, or social groups. The four main castes were the Brahmins, who held the religious power throughout the country; the Kshatriyas, who were both the ruling class and military class; the Vaishyas, consisting of the business community, and finally the Sudras, or workers. Not long after the birth of Siddhartha, Kondanna, a Brahmin, made a prediction that Siddhartha would either become a great ruler or renounce his responsibilities within the ruling class and pursue enlightenment.

By all accounts, Siddhartha led a very sheltered life. The royal family protected him from any kind of real exposure to suffering and anguish. He was always kept at a distance from such suffering so that the royal household could ensure he sustained a privileged and aloof view of society. On a trip into the countryside with Channa, his charioteer, Siddhartha saw a very old man with 'no teeth, sunken cheeks, dry skin, wrinkles, bleary eyes and bent back'.

Then he saw a very sick person lying on the ground, groaning in agony. Next Siddhartha observed a funeral where the mourners were weeping and crying as they carried the lifeless body to the cremation ground. He turned to Channa in utter despair: 'Must everyone I love and myself too simply endure helplessly this tyranny of old age, sickness and death?'

Later, on another trip, he spotted a wandering sage who had renounced the conventional lifestyle to seek wisdom and liberation through simplicity of living and meditation. Siddhartha found himself plunged into depression, turmoil and inner conflict. He lost all interest in his way of life, in living in a world of pleasure and becoming the future King of the Sakyan people.

One night there was yet another major royal function with food, music, dancing, and lavish entertainment for the ruling class. He hated the event and made the decision to run away. That night, upon returning to the palace, he decided that he would abandon all of his duties as a prince, husband and father and try to find a way out of his turmoil. Yet only seven days previously, Siddhartha had become a father when his wife, Princess Yasodhara, the most beautiful woman of the kingdom, gave birth to their son, Rahula.

Haunted by the prospect of having to face ageing, sickness and death, Siddhartha felt the longer his life went on the worse the horror would be. He lost all appetite for wealth, fame and his legendary handsome presence. He regarded them as three terrible karmas. Siddhartha said to himself, 'I must go without seeing my son's face. When I have resolved this suffering I am going through and found a way out of ageing, sickness and death, I shall immediately return to tell Yasodhara and Rahula what I have found.'

Channa took him to the edge of the city where he removed his silk clothes, jewellery and sword and handed these items to his charioteer. He put on some old garments, cut his long hair short and set off walking through the night as the first steps to finding himself and facing up to existence.

For the next six years, Siddhartha spent his time engaged in a whole variety of religious and aesthetic practices to overcome his fears about life. He felt determined to find a genuine liberation that would dissolve the hold over his life of impermanence. He spent time with a celebrated spiritual teacher named Alara Kalama who pointed to a state of Infinite Nothingness as the escape from the world of change and death. Alara invited Siddhartha to teach with him since he also reached that state. Siddhartha realised that he could enter this state through meditation but then would have to go back into the world of suffering.

He then went to visit another famous teacher of meditation called Uddaka Ramaputta. He had gone a step further than Alara Kalama but still Siddhartha knew that Uddaka had not found the fulfilment of the spiritual life. He then pursued his own way. Along with five others he stayed in a hermitage in Sarnath, previously called Uruvela, where they engaged in severe austerities, especially fasting, to overcome any lingering attachment to the body.

Siddhartha gave up trying to rid himself of attachment to the body through this means, left his aesthetic friends and walked for some weeks to another part of the country. He arrived in the village of Bodh Gaya feeling tired and weak. A young woman, named Sujata, saw his condition and offered him a bowl of rice milk. Gaining strength, he spent yet another night in meditation, under a sacred tree beside a nearby river called Neranjara, in one final attempt to awaken fully.

During the night, he recalled sitting under a tree in a field at the age of twelve. He remembered the joy, contentment and calm inner absorption he felt at that time. Now, at the age of thirty-five, he allowed himself to feel that joy once again. During the night, he became exposed to a variety of meditation experiences and then he realised the struggle that human beings face day in and day out. He saw the way people get caught up in their suffering and the conditions leading to that. He realised the dissolution of these conditions and the way for that to happen. All of this became utterly clear to him. He felt an incredible release. He had finally woken up.

He had overcome his inner struggle to make sense of a life that pursued pleasure and privilege to escape the harsh realities of existence. That world of indulging in pleasure and fearing pain totally lost its hold over his existence. He was awake. He was liberated. In addition, he knew that this awakening was available to everybody with the interest and quiet determination to look into the core issues of living.

Siddhartha stayed in the village for the next seven weeks, reflecting on what he had realised. He then made the 170-mile walk back to Sarnath to speak with his friends about his awakening. He explained to them that the extremes of self-hatred and self-gratification inhibited the opportunity for an awakened life.

He then set off to Kapilavastu to see Yasodhara, his wife, and Rahula, his six-year-old son, to tell them that his inner turmoil and depression were completely over. He had discovered the Deathless nature of things so that ageing, sickness and death had ceased to be an issue for him any more. From the time of reconnecting with his son, the Buddha remained a devoted father. The texts record a number of talks with his son on spiritual practice.

From that time on until his death at the age of 80, he walked throughout north India giving teachings and practices to tens of thousands of men, women and children that pointed to a truly liberated and enlightened life. Siddhartha came to be known throughout the region as the 'Awakened One' (the Buddha). Yasodhara and Rahula accompanied him on his long walks with other friends to cities, towns and villages in that region to teach the Dharma of liberation.

Siddhartha died under a tree in Kushinagara after he had eaten some poisonous mushrooms. During his last night on earth, a man came to him to ask him about how he would be able to identify an enlightened teacher. The Buddha advised the man not to concern himself with searching for an enlightened teacher but instead to devote himself to the Dharma of awareness into body, feelings, states of mind and Dharma practices to discover an enlightened life. The Buddha advised the man to work out his liberation with diligence.

Thus ended the life of one of the most remarkable men to have lived on this earth. His voice for a fully enlightened life embraced morality, inquiry, depth of meditation, insight, compassion and a liberating wisdom. Ever since, he has struck a strong chord with countless men and women determined to see through their own experience to what matters most deeply.

The core of his teachings has as much relevance today as it did 2,500 years ago.

May all beings see into the nature of things.
May all beings be awakened.
May all beings be fully liberated.

Daily Meditations

The spiritual life does not have gain, honour and fame for its goal, or the attainment of virtue or the attainment of meditative concentration or knowledge and vision. But unshakeable freedom of mind is the goal of the spiritual life.

Whatever should be done by a compassionate teacher who, out of compassion, seeks the welfare of his students, that I have done for you. These are the roots of trees, these are empty huts. Meditate, do not be negligent, lest you regret it later. This is our instruction to you.

Hatred never ceases by hatred in this world; hatred ceases through non-hatred. This is an endless truth.

One acts in full awareness when eating, drinking, consuming food and tasting. One acts in full awareness when defaecating and urinating. One acts in full awareness when walking, standing, sitting, falling asleep, waking up, talking and keeping silent.

When one is liberated, one knows three unsurpassable qualities: unsurpassable vision, unsurpassable practice and unsurpassable freedom. The Buddha teaches Nirvana and he teaches the Dharma for attaining Nirvana.

These eight worldly conditions keep the world turning around, and the world turns around these eight worldly conditions. What eight?

> Gain and loss,
> Success and failure,
> Praise and blame,
> Pleasure and pain.

They are encountered by an uninstructed worldling, and they are also encountered by an instructed noble student. When an uninstructed worldling comes upon gain, he does not reflect on it thus: 'This gain that has come to me is impermanent, bound up with suffering, subject to change.' He does not know it as it really is. Being thus involved in likes and dislikes, he will not be free from suffering.

An instructed noble student reflects thus: 'This gain that has come to me is impermanent, bound up with suffering, subject to change.' He understands all these things as they really are, and they do not engross his mind.

We will guard the doors of our sense faculties. On seeing a form with the eye, we will not grasp at its signs and features. If we left the eye faculty unguarded, unwholesome states of envy and grief might invade us. We will practise the way of its restraint.

One who looks upon the world as a bubble and a mirage, the King of Death does not see.

Suppose a man were to take a loan and his business were to succeed so that he could repay all the money of the old loan and there would remain enough extra to maintain a wife; then on considering this, he would be glad and full of joy.

Or suppose a man was sent to prison but later he would be released safe and secure, with no loss to his property; then on considering this, he would be glad and full of joy.

So too, when mental hindrances (greed, anger, boredom, worry, doubt) have been abandoned, he experiences that in the same way as freedom from debt or a release from prison.

There are two conditions for the arising of right understanding: the voice of another and wise attention. Right understanding is assisted by five factors when it has liberation by wisdom for its fruit, namely morality, reflection, discussion, calmness and insight.

There are four ways of undertaking things. What are the four?

> There is a way of undertaking things that is pleasant now and ripens in the future as pain.

> There is the way of undertaking things that is painful now and ripens in the future as pain.

> There is the way of undertaking things that is painful now and ripens in the future as pleasant.

> There is the way of undertaking things that is pleasant now and ripens in the future as pleasant.

If there were no Unborn, Unbecoming, Unmade, Unconditioned, no way out would be discerned from what is born, has become, made and conditioned. But since there is an Unborn, Unbecoming, Unmade and Unconditioned, there is a way out.

He abides pervading one quarter with a mind imbued with loving-kindness, likewise the second, likewise the third, likewise the fourth; so above, below, around and everywhere.

And to all, as to himself, he abides pervading the all-encompassing world with a mind imbued with loving-kindness, abundant, exalted, immeasurable, without hostility and without ill will.

It is by living close to a person that his morality is to be known. Then only after a long time, not after a short period; and only by considering that person, not without consideration; and only by one who is wise, not by a fool.

It is by associating with a person that his clarity is to be known.

It is in adversity that a person's fortitude is to be known.

It is by discussion with a person that his wisdom is to be known and then only after a long time, not after a short period.

Having abandoned formal religious practices altogether and actions both 'good' and 'bad', neither longing for 'purity' nor 'impurity', one wanders aloof, abstaining from both without adhering to either extreme.

In every direction there are things you know and recognise, above, below, around and within. Leave them: do not look to them for rest or relief, do not let consciousness dwell on the products of existence, on things that come and go.

Dry up the remains of your past and have nothing for your future. If you do not cling to the present then you can go from place to place in peace.

Udaya asked: 'How does the mindful person bring his mind-flow to an end?'

'The sensations that you feel from the inside have no more fascination for you. And the sensations that you feel from the outside no longer fascinate you. Such a person is mindful and brings his mind-flow to an end.'

Where neither water nor yet earth
Nor fire nor air gain a foothold,
There gleam no stars, no sun sheds light,
There shines no moon,
Yet there no darkness reigns.
When one has come to know this
For oneself, through one's own wisdom,
Then there is freedom from form and formless.

To avoid all evil, to cultivate good and to purify one's mind—this is the teaching of the Buddhas.

There is no meditative concentration for him who lacks insight, and no insight for him who lacks meditative concentration. One who experiences both meditative concentration and insight is indeed close to Nirvana.

Talk that is a help in opening up the mind, and which conduces to complete turning away, peace, direct knowing, enlightenment and Nirvana—that is:

> Talk about fewness of wishes,
>
> Talk about contentment,
>
> Talk about seclusion,
>
> Talk about putting forth energy,
>
> Talk about morality,
>
> Talk about meditative concentration,
>
> Talk about liberation,
>
> Talk about the knowledge and vision of liberation.

Not understanding thoughts,
One runs back and forth with wandering mind.

Though all his life a fool associates with a wise person, he no more comprehends the Truth than a spoon tastes the flavour of the soup.

One is the quest for worldly gain, and quite another is the path to enlightenment. Clearly understanding this, let not a student of the Buddha be carried away by worldly acclaim, but develop non-attachment instead.

Neither mother, father, nor any other relative can do one greater good than one's own well-directed mind.

Those whose minds have reached full excellence in the factors of enlightenment, who, having renounced acquisitiveness, rejoice in not clinging to things—glowing with wisdom, they have attained Nirvana in this very life.

There are two kinds of happiness: the kind to be pursued and the kind to be avoided. When I observed that in the pursuit of such happiness, unwholesome factors increased and wholesome factors decreased, then that happiness was to be avoided.

When I observed that in the pursuit of such happiness unwholesome factors decreased and wholesome ones increased, then that happiness was to be sought after.

Now, there is happiness accompanied by pondering, and happiness not accompanied by it. Of the two, the latter is more excellent. This leads to the cessation of the tendency to project and conceptual proliferation.

It is just as if a man were to say: 'I am going to seek out and love the most beautiful girl in the country.' They might say to him: 'Well, as to this most beautiful girl in the country, do you know whether she belongs to the military, the priestly, the business or the working class?'

He would say: 'No.' Then they might say: 'Well, do you know her name, her family, whether she is tall, short or of medium height, dark, light-complexioned or sallow-skinned, or what village, town or city she comes from?' and he would say: 'No.'

They might say: 'Well then, you don't know or see the one you seek for and desire?' and he would say: 'No.' Does not the talk of that man turn out to be stupid?

The questioner replied: 'Certainly.'

'So it is with those who declare and believe that after death the self is entirely happy and free from disease. Does not their talk turn out to be stupid (since it is only a claim)?'

'Certainly.'

Riches ruin only the foolish, not those in quest of the Beyond.
By craving for riches the witless person ruins himself as well as
others.

What is the Noble Truth of the Way of Practice leading to the Cessation of Suffering? It is just this Noble Eightfold Path, namely:

>Right Understanding
>Right Intention
>Right Speech
>Right Action
>Right Livelihood
>Right Effort
>Right Mindfulness
>Right Meditative Concentration.

What is suffering? Birth is suffering; ageing is suffering; sickness is suffering; death is suffering; sorrow, lamentation, pain, grief, and despair are suffering; not getting what one wants is suffering; losing what one has is suffering; being separated from who and what one loves is suffering. In short, the five aggregates (body, feelings, perceptions, thoughts, consciousness) affected by clinging are suffering.

What are causes of suffering? It is craving, which brings renewal of becoming, is accompanied by infatuation and lust for this and that. There is craving for sensual pleasures, craving for becoming and craving for not becoming.

What is the cessation of suffering? It is the fading away and ceasing, the giving up and letting go of that same craving. This is called the cessation of suffering.

What is Right Understanding? It is the knowledge of suffering, the knowledge of the causes of suffering, the knowledge of the cessation of suffering and the knowledge of the way of practice leading to the cessation of suffering.

What is Right Intention? The intention of letting go, the intention for the absence of ill-will, the intention for the absence of harm.

What is Right Speech? Refraining from lying, refraining from slander, refraining from harsh speech, refraining from frivolous speech.

What is Right Action? Refraining from taking life, refraining from taking what is not given, refraining from sexual misconduct. This is called Right Action.

What is Right Effort? Here, one rouses one's intention, stirs up energy, exerts one's mind and strives to prevent the arising of unarisen evil or unwholesome mental states.

> One exerts one's mind to overcome evil or unwholesome mental states that have arisen.
>
> One exerts one's mind to cultivate unarisen wholesome mental states.
>
> One exerts one's mind to maintain wholesome mental states that have arisen, not to let them fade away, to bring them to greater growth, to fulfillment of development.

What is Right Mindfulness?

> One abides contemplating body as body, ardent, clearly
> aware and mindful, having put aside hankering and
> fretting for the world.
>
> One abides contemplating feelings as feelings.
>
> One abides contemplating states of mind as states
> of mind.
>
> One abides contemplating Dharma as Dharma, ardent,
> clearly aware and mindful, having put aside longing
> and worrying about the world.

What is Right Meditative Concentration?

Secluded from sensual pleasures, secluded from unwholesome states, one enters upon and abides in the first meditative absorption, which is accompanied by applied and sustained reflection, with joy and happiness born of seclusion.

With the subsiding of applied and sustained reflection, by gaining inner calmness and oneness of mind, one enters and remains in the second meditative absorption, born of meditative concentration filled with joy and happiness.

With the fading away of delight, remaining imperturbable, mindful and clearly aware, he experiences in himself the joy of which the Noble Ones say: 'Happy is he who dwells with equanimity and mindfulness', he enters the third meditative absorption.

Having given up pleasure and pain, and with the disappearance of former gladness and sadness, he enters and remains in the fourth meditative absorption which is beyond pleasure and pain, and purified by equanimity and mindfulness.

There are four kinds of verbal conduct not in accordance with the Dharma. Here someone speaks falsehood; when summoned to a court, a meeting, his relatives' presence, royal family's presence, and questioned as a witness. Thus:

Not knowing, he says, 'I know'.

Or knowing, he says, 'I do not know';

Not seeing, he says, 'I see'.

Or seeing, he says, 'I do not see'.

He speaks falsehood for his own ends, or for another's ends, or for some worldly end.

These five trades should not be taken up:

      trading with weapons,

      trading in living beings,

      trading in meat,

      trading in intoxicants,

      and trading in poison.

He who calls others 'a fool' and 'holder of impure Dharma' would indeed invite strife.

When he does not think, 'This is mine' or 'That belongs to them', then, since he has no egoism, he cannot grieve with the thought of 'I do not have'.

'What is it', said Ajita, 'that smothers the world? What makes the world so hard to see? What would you say pollutes the world, and what threatens it most?'

'It is ignorance that smothers the world. It is carelessness and greed that make the world invisible. The hunger of desire pollutes the world, and the fear of the pain of suffering threatens it.'

When a person has assessed the world from top to bottom, when there is nothing in the world that raises a flicker of agitation, then he has become a person free from the tremblings and the hunger of desire. He has become calm. He has gone beyond getting old.

When a person has gone beyond, then there is nothing by which you can measure him or her. That by which he can be talked about is no longer there for him. Yet you cannot say that he does not exist.

All ways of description have been removed.

'I do not say that religious teachers and priests are wrapped in the shroud of birth and ageing,' said the Buddha.

'There are some who have let go of world-views. They have let go of religious practices and rituals, they have left all the different forms behind and they have a total understanding of attachments.

'For them there are no inner poison-drives. These, truly, are the ocean-crossers.'

There is nothing that you need hold on to and there is nothing that you need push away.

There is, in taking things, a thirst, a clinging, a grasping. You must lose it. You must lose it altogether, above, below, around and within. It makes no difference what it is you are grasping at: when you grasp, Mara (the Force of Temptation) stands beside you.

If you are always aware, you will look at the world and see its emptiness. If you give up looking at yourself as a fixed and special identity, then you will have given yourself a way to go beyond death.

Look at the world like this and the King of Death will not see you.

This being, that is; from the arising of this, that arises. That is:

> With ignorance as condition, volitional activities come to be;
>
> With volitional activities as condition, consciousness comes to be;
>
> With consciousness as condition, name-and-form comes to be;
>
> With name-and-form as condition, the sixfold base comes to be;
>
> With the sixfold sense base as condition, contact comes to be;
>
> With contact as condition, feeling comes to be;
>
> With feeling as condition, craving comes to be;
>
> With craving as condition, grasping comes to be;
>
> With grasping as condition, becoming comes to be;
>
> With becoming as condition, birth comes to be;
>
> With birth as condition, ageing and death, sorrow, lamentation, pain, grief and despair come to be.

This is the origin of this whole mass of suffering.

This not being, that is not; from the cessation of this, that ceases.

Not by water is one purified,
Many people bathe in water to be purified.
In whom is Truth and Dharma,
One is purified.

Herein you should train yourself thus:
'In the seen will be merely what is seen;
in the heard will be merely what is heard;
in the sensed will be merely what is sensed;
in the knowing will be merely what is knowing.
Then there will be no here nor there nor in-between. This is the
end of suffering.'

Rahula,

> Develop meditation on loving kindness for ill-will
> will be abandoned.

> Develop meditation on compassion for any cruelty
> will be abandoned.

> Develop meditation on appreciative joy for any
> discontent will be abandoned.

> Develop meditation on equanimity for any aversion
> will be abandoned.

> Develop meditation on foulness for any lust
> will be abandoned.

> Develop meditation on the perception of
> impermanence for the conceit 'I am'
> will be abandoned.

The killing of anger with its poisoned root and
    honeyed tip—
This is the killing that the noble ones praise,
For having slain that, one does not sorrow.

Just as the great ocean has one taste, the taste of salt, so also this Dharma and Discipline has one taste, the taste of liberation.

Rain soddens what is covered up,
It does not sodden what is open.
Therefore uncover what is covered
That the rain will not sodden it.

Practice according to Dharma.
One enjoying the Dharma,
And delighting in the Dharma,
Reflecting upon the Dharma,
Does not fall from the Dharma.

Whether walking or standing,
Sitting or lying down,
With mind inwardly restrained,
He attains to lasting peace.

Even though one might hold on to the hem of my clothes and follow close behind me step by step, if he is envious, negative, corrupt in thought, unmindful, uncomprehending, unconcentrated, of wandering mind and uncontrolled faculties, he is far from me and I am far from him.

What is the reason? Such a person does not see the Dharma. Not seeing the Dharma, he does not see me.

He should so investigate that as he investigates, his consciousness is not distracted and diffused externally. Internally he is not fixed. By not grasping anything one remains undisturbed.

By not grasping anything, there is no coming into existence of birth, ageing, death and suffering in the future.

Joy is non-attachment for one who is content.

Joy is for one who has practised Dharma and sees.

Joy is non-affliction in this world.

Joy is the overcoming of sensual desires.

The abolition of the conceit 'I am'

—that is truly the supreme joy.

If there were no gratification in the world, beings would not become attached to the world. But as there is gratification in the world, beings become attached to it.

If there were no danger in the world, beings would not become disenchanted with the world. But as there is danger in the world, beings become disenchanted with it.

If there were no way out from the world, beings could not escape from the world. But as there is a way out from the world, beings can escape from it.

Victory begets arrogance, the defeated dwell in pain. Happily the peaceful live, discarding both victory and defeat.

Hunger is the worst disease, conditioned things the worst suffering. Knowing this as it really is, the wise realise Nirvana, the highest bliss. Health is the highest gain and contentment the greatest wealth. A trustworthy person is the best relative.

One develops the four bases for spiritual power due to meditative concentration through intention, energy, state of mind and investigation.

Having developed and cultivated the bases for spiritual power, one enters and dwells in the taintless liberation through wisdom.

From attachment springs grief, from attachment springs fear. For him who is wholly free from attachment there is no grief, whence then fear?

Whatever in the world is found in sensual pleasures
And whatever there is of heavenly bliss,
These are not worth a sixteenth part
Of the bliss of craving's destruction.

One follows things that should not be followed and does not follow things that should be followed. It is because one does this that unwished for, undesired, disagreeable things increase and wished for, desired, agreeable things diminish.

Why is that? This is what happens to one who does not see.

Suppose there were a hen with eight or ten or twelve eggs, which she had covered, incubated, and nurtured properly. Even though she did not wish: 'Oh, that my chicks might pierce their shells with the points of their claws and beaks and hatch out safely!' yet the chicks are capable of piercing their shells with the points of their claws and beaks and hatching out safely.

So too, when a noble student has virtue . . . he is called one in higher training who has entered upon the way. His eggs are unspoiled; he is capable of breaking out, capable of enlightenment and attaining the supreme security from bondage.

Rahula,

> Whoever in the past purified their bodily, verbal and mental actions, did so by repeatedly reflecting on their actions.
>
> Whoever in the future will purify their bodily, verbal and mental actions will do so by repeatedly reflecting thus.
>
> Whoever in the present is purifying their bodily, verbal and mental actions does so through repeated reflecting.

Rahula, develop meditation that is like the earth; for when you develop meditation that is like the earth, arisen agreeable and disagreeable contacts will not invade your mind.

Just as people throw clean things and dirty things, excrement, urine, spittle, pus and blood on the earth, and the earth is not horrified, humiliated and disgusted because of that, so too, Rahula, develop meditation that is like the earth.

≽ MARCH 18 ≼

Be a refuge unto oneself.

What have I left undeclared?

> 'The world is eternal'—I have left undeclared.
>
> 'The world is not eternal'—I have left undeclared.
>
> 'The world is finite'—I have left undeclared.
>
> 'The world is infinite'—I have left undeclared.
>
> 'The soul is the same as the body'
>
>   —I have left undeclared.
>
> 'The soul is one thing and the body another'
>
>   —I have left undeclared.
>
> 'After death an enlightened one exists'
>
>   —I have left undeclared.
>
> 'After death an enlightened one does not exist'
>
>   —I have left undeclared.
>
> 'After death One Thus Gone (beyond wanting and
>
>   clinging) both exists and does not exist'
>
>   —I have left undeclared.
>
> 'After death One Thus Gone neither exists nor does
>
>   not exist'—I have left undeclared.

What have I declared?

    'This is suffering'—I have declared.

    'This is the origin of suffering'—I have declared.

    'This is the cessation of suffering'—I have declared.

    'This is the way leading to the cessation of suffering'

      —I have declared.

Men, driven by fear, go for refuge to many places—to hills, woods, trees and shrines. Not by resorting to such a refuge is one released from all suffering.

He who has gone for refuge to the Buddha, the Dharma and the Sangha penetrates with wisdom the Four Noble Truths.

One employs the speech currently used in the world without adhering to it.

I had three palaces, one for the rainy season, one for the winter and one for the summer. I lived in the rains' palace for the four months of the rainy season, enjoying myself with musicians who were all female, and I did not go down to the lower palace.

On a later occasion, having understood as they actually are the origin, the disappearance, the gratification, the danger and the escape in the case of sensual pleasures, I abandoned the pursuit of sensual pleasures, I removed fever for sensual pleasures, and I abide without thirst, with a mind inwardly at peace.

What way is there the preservation of truth? How does one preserve truth?

If a person has a belief, he preserves truth when he says: 'My belief is thus'. He does not yet come to the definite conclusion: 'Only this is true, anything else is wrong'.

In this way, there is the preservation of truth.

When he gives ear, he hears the Dharma. He memorises it and examines the meaning of the teachings he has memorised. When he examines their meaning, he gains a reflective acceptance of those teachings. Zeal springs up.

Having applied his will, he scrutinises. Resolutely striving, he realises with the body the ultimate truth and sees it by penetrating it with wisdom. In this way, there is the discovery of truth.

Form is like a lump of foam,
Feeling like a water bubble;
Perception is like a mirage,
Volitions like a plantain trunk,
And consciousness like an illusion.

There are three searches. The search for pleasure, the search for continued existence and the search for a spiritual life. The Noble Path is to be developed for full understanding of these three searches.

It is by way of elements that beings come together and unite.
   Those with faith unite with those with faith.
   Those concerned with wrong doing unite with those
      similarly concerned.
   And the wise with the wise.

How is there the opinion of a majority? If you cannot settle that dispute in that dwelling place, they should go to a dwelling place where there is a greater number of people. You should all meet together in concord. Then, having met together, the guideline of the Dharma should be drawn out.

Once the guideline of the Dharma has been drawn out, that dispute should be settled in a way that accords with it. Such is the opinion of a majority. And so there comes to be the settlement of some disputes here by the opinion of a majority.

Suppose there were a deadly poisonous snake, and a man came who wanted to live, not to die, and recoiled from pain. What do you think, would that man give that deadly poisonous snake his hand or his thumb, knowing: 'If I am bitten by him I will incur death or deadly suffering'? 'No.'

So too, when one practises restraint throughout the senses and in the mind, having understood that attachment is the root of suffering, one is without attachment.

Ignorance (about suffering) is impermanent, conditioned, dependently arisen, subject to destruction, vanishing, fading away and cessation.

A young tender infant lying prone does not even have the notion 'personality', so how could personality view arise in him? Yet the underlying tendency to personality view lies within him.

A young tender infant lying prone does not even have the notion 'teachings', so how could doubt about teachings arise in him? Yet the underlying tendency to doubt lies within him.

A young tender infant lying prone does not even have the notion 'rules', so how could adherence to rules and observances arise in him? Yet the underlying tendency to adhere to rules and observances lies within him.

A noble student considers thus: 'I am not anything belonging to anyone anywhere, nor is there anything belonging to me in anyone anywhere.'

The priest asked: 'Why is it that some of your students have reached Nirvana and some have not?'

The Buddha replied: 'Are you familiar with the road leading to Rajagaha?'

'Yes, I am familiar with the road leading to Rajagaha.'

'Suppose a man came who wanted to go to Rajagaha, and he approached you and said: 'Venerable sir, I want to go to Rajagaha. Show me the road to Rajagaha.' Then you told him: 'Now, good man, this road goes to Rajagaha. Follow it for awhile and you will see a certain village, go a little further and you will see a certain town, go a little further and you will see Rajagaha with its lovely parks, groves, meadows, and ponds.'

'Then, having been thus advised and instructed by you, he would arrive safely in Rajagaha. Now, since Rajagaha exists and the path leading to Rajagaha exists and you are present as the guide, what is the cause and reason why, when those men have been thus advised and instructed by you, one man takes a wrong road and goes to the west and one arrives safely in Rajagaha?'

'What can I do about that? I am one who shows the way.'

'So too, Nirvana exists and the path leading to Nirvana exists and I am present as the guide.'

With the giving up and relinquishing of clinging to standpoints and underlying tendencies regarding consciousness, I have understood that my mind is liberated.

Here one goes to the forest or to the root of a tree or to an empty hut and sits down. Having folded his legs crosswise, set his body erect and established mindfulness in front of him, mindful he breathes in, mindful he breathes out.

Breathing in long, he understands: 'I breathe in long'; or breathing out long, he understands: 'I breathe out long'.

Breathing in short, he understands: 'I breathe in short'; or breathing out short, he understands: 'I breathe out short'.

He trains thus: 'I shall breathe in experiencing the whole body'; he trains thus: 'I shall breathe out experiencing the whole body'.

He trains thus: 'I shall breathe in tranquillising the bodily formation'; he trains thus: 'I shall breathe out tranquillising the bodily formation'.

He trains thus: 'I shall breathe in experiencing the mind'; he trains thus: 'I shall breathe out experiencing the mind'.

He trains thus: 'I shall breathe in gladdening the mind'; he trains thus: 'I shall breathe out gladdening the mind'.

He trains thus: 'I shall breathe in concentrating the mind'; he trains thus: 'I shall breathe out concentrating the mind'.

He trains thus: 'I shall breathe in liberating the mind'; he trains thus: 'I shall breathe out liberating the mind'.

One reviews this same body up from the soles of the feet and down from the top of the hair, bounded by skin, as full of many kinds of impurity thus: 'In this body there are head-hairs, body-hairs, nails, teeth, skin, flesh, sinews, bones, bone-marrow, kidneys, heart, liver, diaphragm, spleen, lungs, large intestines, small intestines, contents of the stomach, faeces, bile, phlegm, pus, blood, sweat, fat, tears, grease, spittle, snot, oil of the joints and urine.'

How does one revive the past? Thinking, 'I had such material form in the past', one finds delight in that. Thinking, 'I had such feeling in the past' . . . 'I had such perception in the past' . . . 'I had such thoughts in the past' . . . 'I had such consciousness in the past', one finds delight in that.

For the One who has Gone Beyond (limitations) feelings are known as they arise, as they are present, as they disappear; perceptions are known as they arise, as they are present, as they disappear; thoughts are known as they arise, as they are present, as they disappear.

How is it possible that Prince Jayasena, enjoying sensual pleasures, being devoured by thoughts of sensual pleasures, bent on the search for sensual pleasures, could know, see and realise that through letting them go? That is impossible.

Suppose a man needing milk, seeking milk, wandering in search of milk, were to pull a recently-calved cow by her horn. Then, if he made an aspiration or if he made no aspiration, he would still be unable to procure any milk. Why is that? Because that is not the way to procure milk. So too whoever has wrong view is unable to procure any fruit.

≥ APRIL 13 ≤

Let not a person revive the past
Or on the future build his hopes,
For the past has been left behind
And the future has not been reached.
Instead with insight let him see
Each presently arisen state,
Let him know that and be sure of it,
Invincibly, unshakeably.

Today the effort must be made;
Tomorrow death may come, who knows?
No bargain with mortality
Can keep him and his hordes away,
But one who dwells thus ardently,
Relentlessly, by day, by night
It is he, the Peaceful Sage has said,
Who has one auspicious night.

APRIL 15

How does one build up hope upon the future? Thinking, 'I may have such material form in the future', one finds delight in that. Thinking, 'I may have such feeling in the future' . . . 'I may have such perception in the future' . . . 'I may have such thoughts in the future' . . . 'I may have such consciousness in the future', one finds delight in that. That is how one builds up hope upon the future.

When that material form changes and becomes different, his consciousness is preoccupied with the physical changes.

Agitated mental states born of preoccupation with such changes arise together and remain obsessing his mind. Because his mind is obsessed, he is anxious, distressed and concerned.

For the good to do what is good is easy,
For the bad to do what is good is difficult;
For the bad to do what is bad is easy,
For the noble to do what is bad is difficult.

It is by discussion with a person that his or her wisdom is to be known and then only after a long time, not after a short period; and only by considering it, not without consideration; and only by one who is wise, not by a fool.

Some monks and priests
Are deeply attached to their own views;
People who see only one side of things
Engage in quarrels and disputes.

Humanity is attached to self-production
Or holds to production by another.
Those who have not understood this
Have not seen it as a dart.
One who sees clearly
Does not claim, 'I am the doer',
Nor does he claim 'Another is the doer'.
Humanity is possessed by conceit,
Fettered by conceit, bound by conceit,
Speaking vindictively because of their views.

Farmer Bharadvaja said: 'I plough and sow. Having ploughed and sown, I eat. You should plough and sow and then eat. But I see no yoke, nor plough, nor oxen.'

The Buddha replied: 'Confidence is the seed. Self-control is the rein. Wisdom is my yoke and plough. Mindfulness is my goad. Effort is my oxen. I make Truth the destroyer of weeds. My yoked-oxen takes me to Nirvana without stopping. Having accomplished this ploughing, one becomes free from suffering.'

≽ APRIL 22 ≼

'Who craves?'

'Not a valid question,' the Buddha replied. '"Due to what condition does craving arise?" would be a valid question. To this the valid answer is: "With feeling as a condition, craving arises." With craving as condition, clinging comes to be. Such is the origin of this whole mass of suffering.'

If people knew, as I know, the result of giving and sharing, they would not eat a meal without having shared it, nor would they allow the stain of meanness to obsess them and take root in their minds.

Even if it were their last mouthful, they would not eat a meal without having shared it, if there were someone to share it with.

But because people do not know, as I know, the result of giving and sharing, they eat without having given, and the stain of meanness obsesses them and takes root in their minds.

Whatever the reasons for a fortunate rebirth, they do not equal a sixteenth part of the mind-release of loving-kindness. The mind-release of loving-kindness surpasses them and shines, bright and brilliant.

There are two things that cause no remorse. What are the two? Here someone has done what is good, wholesome and beneficial. He has not done evil, callous, wrongful deeds. He is not remorseful on thinking, 'I have done good', and is not remorseful on thinking, 'I have done no evil'.

Where there is an arising of One Thus Gone or no arising, the intrinsic nature still persists, namely the stableness of the Dharma and particular conditionality.

One Thus Gone awakens to it and elucidates on it.

Those of peaceful mind, discerning,
Mindful, given to meditation,
Clearly see things rightly
And do not long for sensual pleasures.
Those peaceful ones, delighting in diligence,
Who see fear in negligence,
Are incapable of falling away
And are close to Nirvana.

Having seen what has come to be
As having come to be,
Passing beyond what has come to be,
They are released in accordance with truth.

Desire and lust for the eye is a corruption of the mind. Desire and lust for the ear, nose, tongue, body and mind is a corruption.

A mind fortified by letting go becomes wieldy in regard to those things that are to be realised by direct knowing.

One should not pursue self-gratification, which is low, vulgar, coarse, ignoble and unbeneficial; and one should not pursue self-hatred, which is painful, ignoble and unbeneficial.

The Middle Way leads to peace, to direct knowing, to enlightenment.

There are four incomprehensibles which if obsessed about would lead to insanity and distress:

> The range of (the mind) of a Buddha
>
> The range of meditative concentration
>
> The results of karma
>
> Speculative views about the world.

These four things are conducive to the growth of wisdom. What four?

> Association with noble persons
>
> Hearing the good Dharma
>
> Wise attention
>
> Practice in accordance with the Dharma

With an unguarded body,
And encumbered by wrong understanding,
Overcome by lethargy and boredom,
One goes along in the power of Mara.

So one should be guarded in mind,
One should make right thought one's domain.
When one has put right view to the forefront
And understood rise and fall
One overcomes lethargy and boredom.

I regard the eye, eye-consciousness, and things cognisable through eye-consciousness thus: 'This is not mine. This I am not. This is not my self.'

I regard the ear . . . the nose . . . the tongue . . . the body . . . the mind, mind-consciousness, and things cognisable thus: 'This is not mine. This I am not. This is not my self.'

There is wavering in one who is dependent;

There is no wavering in one who is independent;

When there is no wavering, there is calmness;

When there is calmness, there is no bias;

When there is no bias, there is no coming and going;

When there is no coming and going, there is no passing
away and reappearing;

When there is no passing away and reappearing, there is
no here nor beyond nor in between.

This is the end of suffering.

Channa used the knife. He is not to be blamed.
(The Buddha's conclusion after the suicide of Channa following his liberation.)

Raindrops on a slightly sloping lotus leaf roll off and do not remain there.

In the same way, when equanimity is established so anything at all, agreeable, disagreeable or both, just as quickly and easily do not remain in the mind.

This is called in the Noble One's Discipline the supreme development of the mental faculties.

Even if bandits were to sever you savagely limb by limb with a two-handled saw, he who gave rise to a mind of hate towards them would not be carrying out my teaching.

I declare that there are two persons one can never repay. What two? One's mother and father. Even if one should carry about one's mother on one shoulder and one's father on the other, and while doing so should live a hundred years, even by that one would not do enough for one's parents.

Even if one were to establish one's parents as the supreme lords and rulers over this earth one would not repay them.

What is the reason for this?

Parents do much for their children: they bring them up, feed them and guide them through this world.

But one who encourages his disbelieving parents, settles and establishes them in faith; who encourages and establishes his immoral parents in virtue; who encourages and establishes his stingy parents in generosity; who encourages and establishes his ignorant parents in wisdom—such a one does enough for his parents. He more than repays them for what they have done.

There are three conditioned marks of the Conditioned. What three? Its arising is discerned, its passing is discerned, its change while persisting is discerned.

There are three unconditioned marks of the Unconditioned. What three? No arising is discerned, no passing is discerned, no change while persisting is discerned.

Two things partake of supreme knowledge. What two? Calmness and insight.

If calmness is developed, what benefit does it bring? The mind becomes developed. And what is the benefit of a developed mind? Running after pleasure is abandoned.

If insight is developed, what benefit does it bring? Wisdom becomes developed. And what is the benefit of developed wisdom? All ignorance is abandoned.

Thus through the fading away of running after pleasure, there is liberation of mind; and through the fading away of ignorance there is liberation by wisdom.

Some misguided people learn the Dharma discourses, verses, sayings and answers to questions—but having learned the Dharma, they do not examine the meaning of these teachings with wisdom. Not examining the meaning of these teachings with wisdom, they do not gain a reflective acceptance of them.

Instead they learn the Dharma only for the sake of criticising others and for winning in debates. They do not experience the good for the sake of which they learned the Dharma. These teachings, being wrongly grasped by them, conduce to their harm and suffering for a long time.

Just as, with an assemblage of parts,
The word 'chariot' is used,
(though a chariot does not exist independently of its
    parts)
So, when the aggregates (body, feelings, perceptions,
    thoughts, consciousness) exist,
There is the convention 'a being' (although a being does
    not exist independently of its parts).

One who is friendly amidst the hostile,
Peaceful amidst the violent
And unattached amidst the attached
—this person I call spiritual.

When walking, he understands: 'I am walking';
When standing, he understands: 'I am standing';
When sitting, he understands: 'I am sitting';
When lying down, he understands: 'I am lying down';
Or he understands accordingly however his body
is used.

One understands contracted mind as contracted mind,
and distracted mind as distracted mind.

One understands exalted mind as exalted mind, and
unexalted mind as unexalted mind.

One understands surpassed mind as surpassed mind,
and unsurpassed mind as unsurpassed mind.

One understands concentrated mind as concentrated
mind, and unconcentrated mind as unconcentrated
mind.

One understands liberated mind as liberated mind, and
unliberated mind as unliberated mind.

By fully understanding the form element
Without getting stuck in the formless,
They are released
And leave death far behind them.

One who does not judge others arbitrarily, but passes judgement impartially, according to truth, that person is a guardian of the Dharma and is called 'just'.

There are these three grounds for making merit. What three?
   The ground for making merit consisting in giving,
   the ground for making merit consisting in virtue,
   and the ground for making merit consisting in
      mental development.

Perceiving what can be expressed through concepts,
Beings take their stand on what is expressed.
Not fully understanding the expressed,
They come under the bondage of Death.

Understanding what is expressed,
The peaceful one delights in the peaceful state.
Standing on Dharma, clearly knowing,
One freely makes use of concepts
But no more enters into the range of concepts.

There are these three kinds of good conduct. What are the three?

Good conduct by body,

good conduct by speech

and good conduct by mind.

Mindfulness is established to the extent necessary for bare knowing. So one abides independent, not clinging to anything in this world.

Whatever person one befriends,
Whomever one associates with,
One becomes of like quality,
One becomes like one's companion.

I have shown you how the Dharma is similar to a raft, being for the purpose of crossing over, not for the purpose of grasping.

When you know the Dharma is similar to a raft, you should abandon even good states, how much more bad states.

How does personality view come to be? Here an untaught ordinary person, who has no regard for noble ones and is unskilled and undisciplined in their Dharma, regards the body as self, or self as possessing a body, or the body is in the self or the self is in the body.

He regards feelings, perceptions, thoughts and consciousness in the same way.

Those dyed in their desires, wrapped in darkness,
Will never discern this abstruse Dharma
Which goes against the worldly stream,
Subtle, deep and difficult to see.

One has realised here and now through direct knowing that unequalled goal of the spiritual life, for the sake of which children from good families rightly go forth from home to the homeless state.

While still young, a black-haired young man endowed with the blessing of youth, in the prime of life, though my mother and father wished otherwise and wept with tearful faces, I shaved off my hair and beard, dressed as a renunciate and went forth from the home life into homelessness.

This generation delights in worldliness, rejoices in it. It is hard for such a generation to see this truth, namely the conditions for dependent arising of phenomena.

It is hard to see this truth, namely, the stilling of all formations, the relinquishing of all attachments.

The development and practice of the perception of impermanence exhausts desire

> for sensual experiences,
> for material forms,
> for becoming and ignorance
> and removes self-pride.

From craving springs grief, from craving springs fear. For him who is wholly free from craving there is no grief, whence then fear?

People hold dear one who embodies virtue and insight, who is principled, has realised the Truth, and who himself does what he ought to be doing.

What has weighed down everything?
What is most extensive?
What is the one thing that has
Everything under its control?

Naming has weighed down everything.
Nothing is more extensive than naming.
Naming is the one thing that has
All under its control.

Thinking himself a lion, the jackal says:
'I'm the king of beasts' and tries to roar
A lion's roar but only howls instead.
Lion is lion and jackal jackal still.

One is not versed in Dharma because one speaks much. One who, after hearing even a little Dharma, does not neglect it but personally realises its truth, is truly versed in the Dharma.

Of all paths the Eightfold Path is the best; of all truths the Four Noble Truths are the best; of all people one who sees clearly is the best.

You yourselves must strive; the Buddhas only point the way. Those meditative ones who tread the path are released from the bonds of Mara.

All conditioned things are impermanent. When one sees this with wisdom one turns away from suffering.

Those who are speculators about the past, the future or both, have fixed views. Such views are merely the feeling of those who do not know and see. They experience these feelings by repeated contact with impressions on the senses and in the mind. These feelings condition desire. Desire conditions clinging (to these speculations).

All conditioned things are unsatisfactory. When one sees this with wisdom one turns away from suffering.

All things are not self—when one sees this with wisdom one turns away from suffering.

Wisdom springs from meditation.
Without meditation wisdom wanes.

Having known these two paths of progress and decline, let a person so conduct himself that his wisdom may increase.

I understand Nirvana, and the path and way leading to Nirvana. I also understand how one who has entered this path will abide in liberation of mind by wisdom by realising for himself through direct knowing, here and now.

On taking refuge in his home from a heavy monsoon, Dhaniya said: 'I dwell near the bank of the river. My house is thatched, the fire is kindled. Rain, O cloud, if you like.'

The Buddha replied: 'I abide near the river bank. My house (body) is uncovered. The fire of desire has gone out. I have passed over the floods to Nirvana.

I have no use of a raft (teachers, teachings, practices). For a long time, my mind has been trained. I am no one's servant. Rain, O cloud, if you like.'

Suppose a man were wounded by an arrow thickly smeared with poison, and his friends and companions, his kinsmen and relatives, brought a surgeon to treat him. The man would say 'I will not let the surgeon pull out this arrow until I know whether the man who wounded me was a priest, businessman or worker.

'I will not let the surgeon pull out the arrow until I know the name, height, skin colour, town or whether he used a long bow or crossbow and what kind of feathers he used and wood for the arrow.'

All of this would not be known to the man so he would die. If anyone should say 'I shall not lead the spiritual life until the Buddha declares to me whether the world is eternal or whether the One Thus Gone exists or not after death', that would remain undeclared and meanwhile the person would die.

What is dependent arising? With birth as condition, ageing-and-death comes to be: whether there is an arising of One Thus Gone (beyond desire) or no arising of such a person, that element still persists, namely specific conditionality.

One Thus Gone awakens to this and breaks through it. Having done so, he explains it and teaches it.

I do not dispute with the world. The world disputes with me. A proclaimer of the Dharma does not dispute with anyone in the world. What is not believed by the wise in the world, of that I say, 'it is not so'. What is believed by the wise in the world, of that I say 'it is so'.

I will teach you Totality. Listen, attend carefully to it and I will speak. Now what is the Totality? It is just the eye and the visible objects, the ear and sounds, the nose and smell, the tongue and tastes, the body and touch, the mind and the objects of mind. This is Totality.

Now, whoever should speak thus: 'Setting aside this Totality, I will proclaim another Totality', it would be mere talk on his part and on being questioned he would be unable to proceed and, in addition, vexation would befall him. For what reason? It would not be within his scope.

The wise see action as it really is. They understand how it dependently arises and are skilled in attending to action and results.

Action makes the world go round. People become bound to their actions like a chariot wheel by a pin.

Perceptions and notions tinged by mental proliferation beset a person. If nothing is found there to hold to, this is the end of the underlying tendency to wanting more and more, to aversion, views, doubt, conceit, becoming and ignorance.

This is the end of resorting to weapons, quarrels, brawls, disputes and revenge.

A person of understanding knows how the senses work in relationship to the mind and the world. The person has gone beyond 'black and white' (duality) and is steadfast. Going beyond all knowledge, one is a person who knows.

I will teach you the end of the path (called)

> The Truth
> The Unaging
> The Stable
> The Undisintegrating
> The Deathless
> The Sublime
> Nirvana
> Freedom
> The Refuge.

What is the freedom of mind through emptiness? One reflects thus: This is empty of self or of what belongs to a self. Unshake-able freedom of mind is empty of greed, hate and delusion.

I will teach you the Dharma for the full understanding of all grasping.

Dependent upon the eye and visible objects visual consciousness arises. Contact is the coming together of these three. Conditioned by contact is feeling. So seeing, the instructed noble student is dispassionate towards the eye, is dispassionate towards objects.

Being dispassionate he is non-attached, being non-attached he is liberated. Being liberated he knows that grasping has been fully understood.

Supposing there were a file of blind men each in touch with the next. The first one does not see, the middle one does not see and the last one does not see. The priests seem to be like a file of blind men. That being so, does not the faith of the priests turn out to be groundless?

Just as a cloth that is defiled and stained becomes pure and bright with the help of clear water, or just as gold becomes pure and bright with the help of a furnace, so too does one of virtue.

Just as a dog bound by a leash tied to a firm post or pillar keeps on running and circling around it, so too people live in fear and disgust of personality. One goes beyond that.

Suppose a man loved a woman with his mind bound to her by intense desire and passion. He might see that woman standing with another man chatting, joking and laughing.

Would not sorrow, pain and despair arise in that man? If he abandoned his desire and lust for her, would sorrow, pain and despair arise in him?

The supreme noble wisdom is the knowing of the destruction of all suffering. This freedom, founded upon truth, is unshakeable. This noble truth, namely Nirvana, has an undeceptive nature.

Whatever is not yours, abandon it. When you have abandoned it, that will lead to your welfare and happiness for a long time.

What is it that is not yours? Material form is not yours. Abandon it. When you have abandoned it, that will lead to your welfare and happiness for a long time.

Having learned the Dharma, they examine the meaning of these teachings with wisdom. They gain a reflective acceptance of them. They do not learn the Dharma for the sake of criticising others. The teachings are conducive to their welfare and happiness for a long time.

A deer-trapper does not lay down bait for a deer herd intending thus: 'May the deer herd enjoy this bait that I have laid down and so be long-lived and handsome and endure for a long time.'

A deer-trapper lays down bait for a deer herd intending thus: 'The deer herd will eat food unwarily by going right in amongst the bait that I have laid down. By so doing they will become intoxicated; they will fall into negligence. I can do with them as I like on account of this bait.'

(In this analogy, 'bait' is a term for sense desire. The deer-trapper is Mara [Temptation].)

One walks without fear,
Stands without fear,
Sits without fear,
Lies down without fear.
Why is that? Because one is out of Mara's range.

Not by observing silence does one become a Sage, if he be foolish and ignorant. The wise one, as if holding a balance for the scales, accepts only the good and rejects the evil. Since he comprehends both, he is called a Sage.

Blind is this world. Here only a few possess insight. Only a few, like birds escaping from a net, go to the realms of joy. Better than sole sovereignty over the Earth, better than going to Heaven, better than lordship over all the worlds, is the fruition of a noble life.

With mind concentrated, he directs and applies his mind to the knowledge of others' minds. He knows and distinguishes with his mind the minds of other people.

From a Dharma student: 'The Buddha has made the Dharma clear in many ways, as though he were turning upright what had been overthrown, revealing what was hidden, showing the way to one who was lost, or holding up a lamp in the dark for those with eyesight to see forms'.

If I think and ponder upon thoughts of letting go, even for a night and day, I see nothing to fear from it. But with excessive thinking and pondering, I might tire my body, and when the body is tired, the mind might become disturbed. It is far from concentration.

So I steadied my mind and concentrated it so that it would not be disturbed.

(A liberated one) will think whatever thought he wishes to think and he will not think any thought that he does not wish to think.

If I am subject to birth, ageing, sickness, death, sorrow and defilements, why should I seek that which is the same?

Just as the footprint of any living being that walks can be placed within the elephant's footprint, so the elephant's footprint is declared the chief of them because of its great size. So too, all wholesome states can be included in the Four Noble Truths.

One who sees dependent arising sees the Dharma. One who sees the Dharma sees dependent arising. And these five aggregates (body, feelings, perceptions, thoughts and consciousness) affected by clinging are dependently arising.

'When you say that the body is my self, do you exercise any such power over that body as to say: "Let my form be thus; let my form not be thus"? If we have no mastery or perfect control over body, how can we call it "myself".'

'Is the body permanent or impermanent?'—'Impermanent.'

'Is what is impermanent unsatisfactory or satisfactory?'—'Unsatisfactory.'

'Is what is impermanent, unsatisfactory and subject to change fit to be regarded thus: "This is mine, this I am, this is my self"?'

'No.'

When he has heard that nothing is worth clinging to, he directly knows everything; having directly known everything he fully understands everything.

Contemplating this, he does not cling to anything in the world. What has to be done has been done. There is no more becoming.

There has never been found a fire which intends, 'Let me burn the fool', but a fool who assaults a fire burns himself by his own doing.

One does not see in unwholesome states the danger, degradation and defilement.

Speculative views are a thicket, a wilderness, beset by suffering and by fever, and do not lead to enlightenment.

One Thus Gone (beyond views) is liberated from reckoning in terms of consciousness. One is profound, immeasurable, unfathomable like the ocean.

Shrouded in darkness, why don't you seek the light?

There are four summaries:

> Any world is unstable; it is swept away,
> Has no shelter and no protector.
> One has to leave all and pass on.
> It is incomplete and cannot be satisfying.

All things get rooted in the will.

All things come to actual existence through attention.

All things arise from contact.

All things meet in feelings.

The foremost of all things is meditative concentration.

All things are mastered by awareness.

Wisdom is the peak of all things.

Liberation is the essence of all things.

All things merge in the Deathless.

Nirvana is the completion of all things.

I undertake the training precept to restrain from killing
   breathing things.

I undertake the training precept to abstain from taking
   what is not given.

I undertake the training precept to abstain from
   causing sexual harm.

I undertaking the training precept to abstain from
   speaking lies.

I undertake the training precept to abstain from
   heedlessness due to intoxicants.

This is the Deathless, namely, the liberation of the mind through not clinging.

What kind of acquisition of view causes unwholesome states to increase and wholesome states to diminish?

> There is nothing given (to others),
>
> Nor anything offered,
>
> Nor personal sacrifices made,
>
> Nor belief in the results of good or bad actions.

For in whatever way they conceive of anything, the fact is ever other than that.

Just as a line drawn on water with a stick will quickly vanish and will not last long; even so is human life like a line drawn on water. It is short. For none who is born can escape death.

It can be expected that one (of Dharma practice) enters upon and abides in the deliverance of mind that is temporary or the freedom that is perpetual and unshakeable.

These six things rarely appear in the world:

> Rare in the world is the appearance of One Thus Gone
> (beyond desire).
>
> Rare in the world is the appearance of one who teaches
> the Dharma and Discipline proclaimed by One
> Thus Gone.
>
> Rare in the world is it to be reborn in the land of the
> noble ones.
>
> Rare in the world is the possession of unimpaired
> physical and mental faculties.
>
> Rare in the world is absence of stupidity and dullness.
>
> Rare in the world is a desire for wholesome qualities.

Said Pingiyani: Just as a capable physician might instantly cure a patient who is in pain and gravely ill; so too, dear sir, whatever one hears of Gautama's Dharma, be it discourses, mixed prose, explanations or marvellous accounts, one's sorrow, grief and despair will vanish.

If one can find a worthy friend, then walk with him, content and mindful. If one finds no worthy friend, then as a king leaves his conquered realm, walk in the woods alone.

Better to walk alone than with fools.

For one who is virtuous and endowed with virtue, there is no need for an act of will so that non-remorse arise in me. It is a natural law that non-remorse will arise in one who is virtuous.

For one free of remorse, there is no need for an act of will so that gladness will arise in me. It is a natural law that gladness will arise in one who is free from remorse.

One directly knows Nirvana as Nirvana.

One does not conceive of oneself as one with Nirvana.

One does not conceive of oneself as in Nirvana.

One does not conceive of oneself apart from Nirvana.

Why is that? So that one may fully understand it.

I will teach you the Dharma for the full understanding of all grasping.

Dependent upon the eye and visible objects visual consciousness arises. Contact is the coming together of these three. Conditioned by contact is feeling. So seeing, the instructed noble student is dispassionate towards the eye, is dispassionate, towards objects etc.

Being dispassionate he is non-attached, being non-attached he is liberated, being liberated he knows that grasping has been fully understood.

Friends, who declare before me that they have attained the final knowledge of arahantship, all these do so in one of four ways. What four?

> One develops insight followed by calmness so the path arises within.
>
> One develops calmness followed by insight so the path arises within.
>
> One develops calmness and insight together.
>
> One develops and cultivates that path, and while doing so problems are abandoned and the underlying tendencies eliminated. So there comes a time when the mind becomes internally steadied, composed, unified and concentrated.

Who declare they have attained the final knowing of arahantship, all these do so in one of these four ways.

The other person is given to anger and revenge and he is firmly attached to his views. I cannot make that person emerge from the unwholesome and establish him in the wholesome. One should not underrate equanimity towards such a person.

Meditating on the not-beautiful should be cultivated for overcoming lust;

Loving kindness should be cultivated for overcoming negativity;

Mindfulness of breathing should be cultivated for cutting off (discursive) thinking;

The perception of impermanence should be cultivated for the removal of the conceit 'I am'.

While still an unenlightened bodhisattva,
I searched the four quarters of the universe
 with my mind
And found no one dearer to me than myself.
So likewise each person is to himself most dear.
Who loves oneself can never harm another.

Having slain mother (craving), father (conceit), two warrior kings (duality) and destroyed a country (sense organs and sense objects) together with its treasurer (attachment and lust), ungrieving goes the spiritual person.

Those students of Gautama always awaken happily who day and night constantly practise the recollection of the Buddha.

Those students of Gautama always awaken happily who day and night constantly practise the recollection of the Dharma.

Those students of Gautama always awaken happily who day and night constantly practise the recollection of the Sangha.

Those students of Gautama always awaken happily whose minds by day and night delight in the practice of non-harming.

Those students of Gautama always awaken happily whose minds by day and night delight in the practice of meditation.

⮞ AUGUST 7 ⮜

What is clinging? There are these four kinds of clinging:

    Clinging to pleasure

    Clinging to views

    Clinging to rules, techniques and vows

    Clinging to self.

Let go of the past, let go of the future, let go of the present, and cross over to the farther shore of existence. With mind wholly liberated, you shall come no more to birth and death.

To teach the Dharma to others one should set up in oneself five standards for doing so. What five?

> I shall give a gradual discourse in that way the Dharma should be taught to others.
>
> I shall give a well-reasoned discourse.
>
> Moved by sympathy I shall speak.
>
> Not for the sake of worldly advantage, I shall speak.
>
> Without alluding to myself or to others, I shall speak.

It is not easy to teach the Dharma to others. When doing so one should set up in oneself these five standards.

For one who is a Dharma student
There is no other thing so helpful
For reaching the highest goal
As the factor of wise attention.

He for whom there is neither this shore nor the other shore, nor yet both, he who is free of cares and is unfettered—him do I call a spiritual person.

Some declare the self to be:

> Material and limited
>
> Material and unlimited
>
> Immaterial and limited
>
> Immaterial and unlimited.

Having seen the attraction and the peril in such views, one is freed without attachment. This is to be liberated by wisdom.

This world is subject to torment;
Afflicted by contact, it calls a disease 'self'.

Whoever has said that freedom from becoming comes about through some kind of becoming, none of them, I say, are free from becoming.

Whoever has said that escape from becoming comes about through non-becoming, none of them, I say, have escaped from becoming.

This suffering arises dependent upon clinging. With the ending of all grasping, no suffering is produced.

Said Ananda: Half of this spiritual life is friendship with the good, companionship with the good, association with the good.

The Buddha replied: Do not say that, Ananda. The whole of this spiritual life is friendship with the good, companionship with the good, association with the good.

One who is a friend cultivates and seriously practises the Noble Eightfold Path.

The streams of tears that we have shed as we journey through this existence, through being united with the disagreeable and separated from the agreeable, is more than the water in the great oceans.

Trivial thoughts, subtle thoughts,
Mental jerkings that follow one along:
Not understanding these mental thoughts,
One runs back and forth with wandering mind.

But having known these mental thoughts,
The ardent and mindful one restrains them.
An awakened one has entirely abandoned them,
These mental jerkings that follow one along.

Unattached to things that arouse attachment,
Unangered by things that provoke anger,
When his mind is cultivated thus
How can suffering come to him?

For the good to do what is good is easy,
For the bad to do what is good is difficult;
For the bad to do what is bad is easy,
For the noble to do what is bad is difficult.

For you who enjoy living at home with the encumbrance of children, making use of sandalwood from Varanasi, wearing garlands and scents, handling gold and silver, it is difficult for you to know whether or not someone is fully liberated or whether they have entered the path to being fully liberated.

Just as a solid rock is not shaken by the storm, even so the wise are not affected by praise or blame.

One should not be another's man.
One should not live depending on another.
One should not make a business of Dharma.

With mind concentrated, purified, clear and established, he directs and inclines it towards knowing and seeing. And he knows: This my body is material, made up from the four great elements, born of mother and father, fed on rice and gruel, impermanent, liable to be injured and abraded, broken and destroyed, and this is my consciousness which is bound to it and dependent on it.

All tremble at violence, all fear death. Putting oneself in the place of another, one should not kill nor cause another to kill.

All conditioned things are impermanent.
All conditioned things are unsatisfactory.
All conditioned things are not self (not I, not myself).

Behold this Dharma hard to comprehend.
Here the unwise are bewildered.
For those with blocked minds it is obscure,
Sheer darkness for those who do not see.

Who else apart from the noble ones
Are able to understand this state (of liberation)?
When they have rightly known that state
They are fully quenched.

Before long, alas! this body will lie upon the earth, unheeded and lifeless, like a useless log.

Whatever harm an enemy may do to an enemy, or a hater to a hater, an ill-directed mind inflicts on oneself a greater harm.

Realising that this body is like froth, penetrating its mirage-like nature, and plucking out Mara's flower-tipped arrows, go beyond sight of the King of Death!

The fool worries, thinking, 'I have sons, I have wealth'. Indeed, he does not own a self. How could he own sons? How could he own wealth?

Eating, drinking, chewing and savouring end in excrement and urine; this is their outcome.

And what is the diversity of suffering? There is intense suffering and moderate suffering. There is suffering that fades away slowly and suffering that fades away quickly.

There is that base where there is no earth, no water, no fire, no air; no base consisting of infinite space, infinite consciousness, infinite nothingness; neither-perception-nor-non-perception; neither this world nor another world nor both.

Here I say there is no coming, no going, no staying, no deceasing, no arising. Not fixed, not movable, it has no support. Just this is the end of suffering.

To arouse energy one reflects 'let the flesh and blood dry up in my body but I will not stop until I have attained what can be attained'.

The lazy person dwells in dissatisfaction, soiled by unhealthy states of mind and great is the personal good that he or she neglects. Arouse your energy. Thus you should train yourselves. Strive with diligence.

The one who only takes for himself can be seen to be a false friend for four reasons:

>He takes everything.

>He wants a lot for very little.

>What he must do he does out of fear.

>He seeks his own ends.

What use is there for a well
If there is water everywhere?
When craving's root is severed
What should one go about seeking?

On seeing a visible object with the eye, one does not grasp at its major signs or secondary characteristics. Because greed and sorrow, unskilled states, would overwhelm one.

So he practises guarding it, he protects the eye-faculty, develops restraint. He experiences within himself the blameless joy that comes from maintaining this guarding of the faculties.

And when he knows that these five hindrances have left him, gladness arises in him, from gladness comes delight, from the delight in his mind his body is tranquillised. With a tranquil body he feels joy, and with joy his mind is concentrated.

The gift of Dharma excels all gifts.
The taste of Dharma excels all tastes.
The delight in Dharma excels all delights.

Who is called 'prosperous'?

One who cultivated the seven factors for enlightenment, namely:

> Mindfulness
>
> Enquiry
>
> Energy
>
> Joy
>
> Calmness
>
> Meditative Concentration and Equanimity.

Such a person is called prosperous.

With mind concentrated, he applies and directs his mind to the knowledge of others' minds.

He knows and distinguishes with his mind the minds of others.

He knows the mind with passion to be with passion.

He knows the mind without passion to be without passion, the mind with hate and the mind without hate.

This world for the most part depends upon a duality of existence and non-existence.

For one who sees the arising of the world as it really is with wisdom, there is no notion of non-existence in regard to the world.

For one who sees the cessation of the world as it really is with correct wisdom, there is no notion of existence in regard to the world.

Just as if a mighty trumpeter were with little difficulty to make a proclamation to the four quarters, so by this meditation, by this liberation of the heart through loving-kindness, he leaves nothing untouched, nothing unaffected in the sensuous sphere.

In this matter, those who say one's perceptions arise and cease without cause or condition are totally mistaken.

Why is that? One's perceptions arise and cease owing to a cause and conditions.

To hear those who have morality, meditative concentration, wisdom, liberation, knowledge and insight of liberation is of great profit.

One living mindfully considers with wisdom, investigates and undertakes an inquiry into the Dharma. At that time the enlightenment factor of inquiry is aroused.

How does one engage in clear comprehension? Feelings are known as they arise, stay and come to an end. Thoughts are known as they arise, stay and come to an end. Perceptions are known as they arise, stay and come to an end.

One should live mindful and with clear comprehension. This is our instruction to you.

When one has good friends,
And is reverential and respectful,
Doing what one's friends advise,
Clearly comprehending and mindful,
One may progressively attain
The destruction of all problems.

It is the rule that when a buddha-to-be has entered his mother's womb, his mother by nature becomes virtuous.

It is the rule that when a buddha-to-be has entered his mother's womb, she cannot be overcome by a man with lustful thoughts.

It is the rule when the buddha-to-be issues from his mother's womb, angels welcome him first, then humans.

Feeling conditions craving,
Craving conditions seeking,
Seeking conditions acquisition,
Acquisition conditions decision-making,
Decision-making conditions desire,
Desire conditions attachment,
Attachment conditions appropriation,
Appropriation conditions possessiveness,
Possessiveness conditions guarding of possessions,
and so arises the taking up of evil
and unskilled states.

One who says: 'Feeling is my self' should be told: 'There are three kinds of feeling, friend: pleasant, painful and neutral. Which of the three do you consider to be self?'

When a pleasant feeling is felt, no painful or neutral feeling is felt, but only pleasant feeling.

When a painful feeling is felt, no pleasant or neutral feeling is felt, but only painful feeling.

And when a neutral feeling is felt, no pleasant or painful feeling is felt, but only neutral feeling.

O house-builder, you are seen! You will not build this house again. For your rafters are broken and your ridgepole shattered. My mind has reached the Unconditioned: I have attained the destruction of craving.

I hope that you are all living in concord, with mutual appreciation, without disputing, blending like milk and water, viewing each other with kindly eyes.

Material form is impermanent, feeling is impermanent, perception is impermanent, thoughts are impermanent, consciousness is impermanent.

Our livelihood shall be purified, clear and open, flawless and restrained, and we will not laud ourselves and disparage others on account of that purified livelihood.

When you say thus: 'Feeling is my self', do you exercise any power over that feeling as to say: 'Let my feeling be thus; let my feeling not be thus'?

'No.'

We will be moderate in eating. Reflecting wisely, we will take food neither for amusement nor for intoxication nor for the sake of physical beauty and attractiveness, but only for the endurance and continuance of this body, for ending discomfort and for assisting the spiritual life.

With the divine eye, one sees beings passing away and reappearing, inferior and superior, fair and ugly, fortunate and unfortunate, and one understands how beings pass on according to their actions.

Just as though there were two houses with doors and a man with good sight standing there between them saw people entering the houses and coming out and passing to and fro.

Just as if there were a lake in a mountain recess, clear and undisturbed, so that a man with good sight standing on the bank could see shells, gravel and pebbles, and also shoals of fish swimming about and resting.

So too, one understands as it actually is: This is suffering, the origin, the cessation and the way.

(The Buddha) teaches the Dharma good in the beginning, good in the middle and good in the end, with the right meaning and phrasing, and he reveals a spiritual life that is utterly perfect and pure.

The footprints of all living beings that walk fit into the footprint of the elephant.

So too, all the steps that lead to enlightenment, the faculty of wisdom is declared to be their chief.

If one encounters the Dharma and discipline and develops loving-kindness, compassion, appreciative joy and equanimity and finds internal peace, then that person practises the proper way.

Pleasant feeling is impermanent, conditioned, neutral, dependently arisen, bound to decay, to fade away, to cease—and so too are painful feeling and feelings—neither pleasant nor unpleasant.

So anyone who, on experiencing a pleasant feeling, thinks: 'This is my self', must, at the cessation of that pleasant feeling, think: 'My self has gone!' and the same with painful feelings or feelings neither pleasant nor unpleasant.

Whoever thinks: 'Feeling is my self' is contemplating something in this present life that is impermanent, a mixture of happiness and unhappiness, subject to arising and passing away. Therefore it is not fitting to maintain: 'Feeling is my self'.

When they want to cross the sea, the lake or pond, people make a bridge or raft—the wise have crossed already.

The mind imbued with wisdom becomes completely free from the corruptions, that is, from the corruption of sensuality, of becoming, of false views and of ignorance.

Enter upon and abide in pure, supreme Emptiness.

Mindfulness is simply established to the extent necessary for bare knowing and mindfulness. One abides independent, not clinging to anything in the world.

A noble student has unwavering confidence in the Buddha.

A noble student has unwavering faith in the Dharma, thus: Well-proclaimed by the Buddha is the Dharma, visible here and now, timeless, inviting inspection, leading onward, to be comprehended by the wise each one for himself. A noble student has unwavering confidence in the Sangha, thus: Well-directed is the Sangha of the Buddha's students, of upright conduct, on the right path.

The Sangha has morality dear to the Noble Ones, unbroken, uncorrupted, conducive to meditative concentration and is liberating.

I have taught the Dharma making no 'inner' and 'outer'. The One Thus Gone has no 'teacher's fist' in respect of teachings.

If there is anyone who thinks: 'I shall take charge of the order', or 'The order should refer to me', let him make some statement about the order, but I do not think in such terms.

Ripe in years. My life-span is determined.
Now I go from you.
Be untiring, mindful, disciplined,
Guarding your minds with well-collected thought.
He who, tireless, keeps to the Dharma and discipline,
Leaving birth behind will put an end to woe.

It may be that you will think: The teacher's instruction has ceased. It should not be seen like this, for what I have taught and explained to you as Dharma and discipline will, at my passing, be your teacher.

There are six dangers attached to addiction to strong drink and
sloth-producing drugs:

>Waste of money
>
>Increased quarrelling
>
>Liability to sickness
>
>Loss of good name
>
>Indecent exposure of what one says and does
>
>Weakening of intellect.

Do not die filled with longing. To die filled with longing is painful.

Magha asked: 'I make donations, I give financial support. I am an approachable person and open to requests. The wealth I give away I made quite lawfully. Do these donations produce merit for me?'

The Buddha replied: 'These gifts and offerings are certainly worthwhile and do produce great merit. In the enjoyment of meditation, in the fullness of knowledge, in the strength of mindfulness, people find full enlightenment and are a shelter for many. When the time comes for giving gifts, these are the people to give to.'

Mind precedes all mental states. Mind is their chief; they are all mind-wrought. If a person speaks or acts with an impure mind, suffering follows him as the wheel follows the foot of the ox.

Mind is their chief; they are all mind-wrought. If with a pure mind a person speaks or acts, happiness follows him like his never-departing shadow.

Those who mistake the unessential to be essential and the essential to be unessential, dwelling in mistaken thoughts, never arrive at the essential.

Just as the rain breaks through an ill-thatched house, even so inflamed passion penetrates an undeveloped mind.

Much though he recites the sacred texts, but acts not accordingly, he does not partake of the blessings of a spiritual life. That heedless man is like a cattle farmer who only counts the cows of others.

Wisdom and consciousness, friend—these states are conjoined, not disjoined, and it is impossible to separate each of these states from the other in order to describe the difference between them.

For what one wisely understands, that one cognises, and what one cognises, that one wisely understands.

Unification of mind is meditative concentration.

There are seven underlying tendencies:

> Desire
>
> Aversion
>
> Views
>
> Doubt
>
> Conceit
>
> Holding onto existence
>
> Ignorance.

This path is developed for the full understanding and abandoning of these tendencies.

May all beings be happy and secure!
May their hearts be wholesome!
Whatever living beings there may be:
Weak or strong, tall or middling,
Short or large, without exception;
Seen or unseen, dwelling far or near,
Already born or yet to be born,
May all beings be happy!

One should cultivate an unlimited loving mind
Without obstruction, anger or opposition
To the whole world
Above, below and across.

One does not repeat elsewhere what one has heard in order to divide. One reunites those who are divided, a promoter of friendships, who enjoys concord, rejoices in concord, delights in concord, a speaker of words that promote concord.

> Abandoning harsh speech, one abstains from harsh speech.
>
> One speaks such words as are gentle, pleasing to the ear and loveable.
>
> One speaks such words as go to the heart, are courteous, desired by many and agreeable to many.
>
> Abandoning gossip, one abstains from gossip.
>
> One speaks at the right time,
>
> Speaks what is fact,
>
> Speaks on what is good,
>
> Speaks on the Dharma and the Discipline at the right time.
>
> One speaks such words as are worth recording, reasonable, moderate and beneficial.

Heat is generated and fire is produced from the friction of two fire-sticks, but when the sticks are separated the heat then ceases and subsides.

So with the cessation of painful contact, the corresponding feelings can cease and subside.

Desire is a maker of measurement,
hate is a maker of measurement,
and delusion is a maker of measurement.
The freedom of mind that is unshakeable is empty of
measurement.

I do not perceive any single hindrance other than the hindrance of ignorance. Obstructed through ignorance, humankind wanders on for a long time.

Live enjoying seclusion.
Mindful, given to meditation,
Clearly see things.
Delight in diligence.
One is close to Nirvana.

Go and travel for the welfare of the many, happiness of the many, out of compassion, for the benefit and happiness of gods and humans.

Teach the Dharma that is beneficial in the beginning, middle and end.

One turns one's mind away from those states and directs it towards the deathless element.

This is the way.

What is the diversity of karma? There is karma leading to the hells, to the animal realm, to the sphere of ghosts, to the human world and to the heavenly realms.

If you see your own benefit, then make the effort.
If you see another's benefit, then make the effort.
If you see benefit for both, then make the effort.

These teachings of One Thus Gone are profound, deep in meaning, transcendent and connected with Emptiness.

There are six dangers attached to gambling:

> The winner makes enemies.
> The loser bewails his loss.
> One wastes one's present wealth.
> One's word is not trusted.
> One is despised by one's friends.
> One is not wanted in marriage.

Truth is one. There is no second.

Through seeing clearly the process of dependent arising, one abandons such uncertainties about oneself as:

> Was I in the past? Was I not in the past?
> What was I in the past? How was I in the past?
> Having been what, what was I in the past?

> Shall I be in the future? Shall I not be in the future?
> What shall I be in the future? How shall I be in the future?
> Having been what, what shall I be in the future?

> Am I? Am I not? What am I? How am I?
> Where have I come from? Where am I going?

When one sees the benefits, it should be enough for him to establish the perception of non-self in all things without exception.

> Notions of 'I' will dissolve.
>
> Notions of 'mine' will dissolve.
>
> One shall be endowed with uncommon knowledge.
>
> One shall clearly understand causes and the
>
>   phenomena arisen from causes.

Why was it said: this Dharma is for one of vigilant mindfulness, not for one of lax mindfulness? Here, one who is mindful, equipped with the keenest mindfulness and reflection; he remembers well and keeps in mind what has been said and done long ago.

The one who is without blind faith, who knows the Uncreated, who has severed all links, who has destroyed all causes (for karma) and who has thrown out all desires—he truly is the most excellent of persons.

Inspiring are the forests where worldly people find no pleasure.
There the undemanding rejoice.

Better than reciting a hundred meaningless verses is the reciting of one verse of Dharma, hearing which one attains peace.

Better it is to live one day virtuous and meditative than to live a hundred years immoral and uncontrolled.

Better it is to live one day seeing the rise and fall of things than to live a hundred years without ever seeing the rise and fall of things.

Better it is to live one day seeing the Deathless than to live a hundred years without ever seeing the Deathless.

Better it is to live one day seeing the Supreme Truth than to live a hundred years without ever seeing the Supreme Truth.

Think not lightly of evil, saying, 'It will not come to me'. Drop by drop is the water pot filled; likewise, the fool, gathering it little by little, fills himself with evil.

Think not lightly of good, saying, 'It will not come to me'. Drop by drop is the water pot filled; likewise, the wise person, gathering it little by little, fills himself with good.

There are five ways teachers minister to their students:

> They give thorough instruction.
>
> Make sure they have understood what needs
> to be understood.
>
> Give them a thorough grounding in all the
> necessary skills.
>
> Recommend their students to others.
>
> Enable them to feel secure.

If the hand has no wound, one may even carry poison in it. Poison does not affect those free from wounds. Evil does not affect those who carry no evil.

Neither in the sky nor in mid-ocean, nor by entering into mountain clefts, nowhere in the world is there a place where one may escape from the results of evil deeds.

In a grove of trees, the Buddha took up a few leaves in his hand and said: 'What do you think is more numerous? These few leaves that I have taken up in my hand or those in the grove overhead?

'The leaves taken up in the hand are few, but those in the grove overhead are numerous.

'So too, the things I have directly known but have not taught you are numerous, while the things I have taught you are few. And why have I not taught those many things? Because they are irrelevant to the fundamentals of the spiritual life, not leading to direct knowing of enlightenment.

'And what have I taught? I have taught: "This is suffering; its causes, its cessation and the way leading to its cessation." And why have I taught this? Because this is beneficial, relevant to the fundamentals of the spiritual life, to peace, to enlightenment and Nirvana.'

What is the diversity of feelings?

> There are pleasant feelings that are worldly or
> spiritual.
>
> There are unpleasant feelings that are worldly or
> spiritual.
>
> There are feelings that are neither unpleasant nor
> pleasant that are worldly or spiritual.

A noble student knows the conditioned arising, the diversity and outcome of feelings.

Just as a rocky mountain is not moved by storms,
So sights, sounds, tastes, smells, contacts and ideas,
Whether desirable or undesirable,
Will never stir one of steady nature,
Whose mind is firm and free.

Therefore, friends, you should train yourselves thus: though we ourselves are joined to the Dharma (Dharma-yogis), we will praise also those who are meditators. And why?

Such outstanding people are rare in the world who have personal experience of the deathless element.

And the others should train themselves thus: though we ourselves are meditators, we will praise also those who are Dharma-yogis.

And why? Such outstanding persons are rare in the world who can by their wisdom clearly understand a difficult subject.

Punnaka asked, 'Why do people make offerings to priests, rulers and their God?'

The Buddha: 'People make offerings because they want to preserve their lives as they were. Their prayers, praises and offerings were all made on the basis of reward.

'But they cannot go beyond getting old (through prayers). When a person has assessed this world from top to bottom then he becomes free from its fumes and goes beyond old age.'

A tangle inside, a tangle outside,
This generation is entangled in a tangle.
I ask you this, O Gautama,
Who can disentangle this tangle?

One established in virtue, wise,
Developing the mind and wisdom,
Who is ardent and discreet
Can disentangle this tangle.

The world's end can never be reached
By means of travelling,
Yet without reaching the world's end
There is no release from suffering.

Therefore, truly, the world-knower, the wise one,
Gone to the world's end, fulfiller of the spiritual life,
Having known the world's end, at peace,
Longs not for this world or another.

Just as mountains of solid rock,
Massive, reaching to the sky,
Might draw together from all sides,
Crushing all in the four quarters—
So ageing and death come,
Rolling over living beings—
They spare none along the way
But come crushing everything.

There's no ground there for elephant troops,
For chariot troops and infantry.
One can't defeat them by subterfuge,
Or buy them off by means of wealth.
Therefore a person of wisdom here,
Out of regard for his own good,
Steadfast, should settle faith
In the Buddha, Dharma and Sangha.

A naked ascetic, Kassapa, asked: 'Is suffering created by oneself?'

The Buddha replied, 'Not so.'

'Is suffering created by another?'

'Not so.'

'Is suffering created by oneself and another?'

'Not so. But there is suffering. Without veering towards extremes of self and other, there is the teaching of the middle way. With ignorance as a condition, volitional formations arise leading to the whole mass of suffering.'

Having traversed all quarters with the mind,
One finds none anywhere dearer than oneself.
Likewise, each person holds himself most dear;
Hence one who loves himself should not harm others.

Freedom of mind of loving kindness has inner beauty as the highest.

Freedom of mind of compassion has infinite space as the highest.

Freedom of mind of appreciative joy has infinite consciousness as the highest.

Freedom of mind of equanimity has no-thingness as the highest.

By what is the world led around?
The world is led around by the mind.

Feelings (including emotions) should be known. The conditions and causes for feelings should be known, their diversity and their outcome as well.

I shall teach you the Unconditioned and the way leading to the Unconditioned.

What are the four causes of evil from which one refrains?
Evil springs from

> attachment,
> ill-will,
> folly
> and fear.

One who truly sees suffering also sees the causes of suffering, sees the cessation of suffering and the way leading to the cessation of suffering.

One who truly sees the causes of suffering also sees suffering, the cessation of suffering and the way leading to the cessation of suffering.

One who truly sees the cessation of suffering also sees suffering, the causes of suffering and the way leading to the cessation of suffering.

One who truly sees the way leading to the cessation of suffering, sees suffering, the causes of suffering and the cessation of suffering.

When this noble student has made his mind free of hatred, free of ill will and uncorrupted, he has won these assurances in this very life.

If there is another world, and if good and bad deeds bear fruit and yield results, it is possible that with the break-up of the body after death, I shall arise in a good destination, in a heavenly world.

If there is no other world, and if good and bad deeds do not bear fruit and yield such results, then here in this very life, I live happily, free of hatred and ill will.

It's only dissatisfaction that comes to be,
Dissatisfaction that arises and falls away.
Nothing but dissatisfaction comes to be,
Nothing but dissatisfaction ceases.

There are three ways of making merit. What three? There are ways of making merit by giving, by virtue and by the development of meditation.

I see no other thing that is so quickly transformed as the mind.

For it is a sign of growth in the Discipline of the Noble One that one recognises one's offence, makes amends for it according to the rule, and in future practises restraint.

The Sangha (upholders of the Dharma) is fit for gifts, hospitality, offerings, respect and is an incomparable field of merit for the world.

Not the sweet smell of flowers, not even the fragrance of jasmine, blows against the wind. But the fragrance of virtuous people pervades all directions through the fragrance of their virtue.

You are the owner of your deeds,
Heir of your deeds,
Having deeds as your parents,
Deeds as your family,
Deeds as your refuge,
You will become heirs of whatever you do.

As soon as meditative concentration has been developed by you and frequently practised, then you should train thus:

I will develop freedom of mind for loving kindness and compassion.

It is good

To abide from time to time in perceiving the non-beautiful in the beautiful,

To abide from time to time in perceiving the beautiful in the non-beautiful.

For what reason to see the non-beautiful in the beautiful?

So that no lust arises in me.

For what reason to see the beautiful in the non-beautiful?

So that no hate arises in me.

For what reason should one overcome the beautiful and non-beautiful?

So that one remains mindful, with clear comprehension and equanimity.

There are five ways of getting rid of a grudge. What five?

If a grudge arises towards any person, then one should culti-vate loving-kindness, compassion or equanimity towards him.

Or one should pay no attention to him and give no thought to him. In that way one can remove the grudge.

Or one may apply to that person the fact of ownership of karma: 'This worthy person is the owner of his actions and the heir of his actions; whatever he does, good or bad, he will be heir to that.'

The tears and anguish that follow arguments and quarrels, the arrogance, pride, grudges and insults that go with them, are all the result of one thing. They come from holding things precious and dear.

When he thinks of letting go, giving up, he feels an urge towards this and inclines to it, his mind is well directed. Then his mind rises above this pursuing of pleasure, ill will, violence, material things and obsession with personality.

When thinking of material things, he feels no urge towards them, nor dwells on them so that he rises above such thinking.

When thinking of renunciation and letting go, he feels an urge towards this so that his mind is well directed and well developed.

Through elimination of conceit around such matters, he puts an end to problems.

What is the gain unsurpassed? Some gain a child, a wife, wealth, this or that; or else they gain faith in an ascetic or priest of wrong views. I say it is not gain.

It is gain that is unsurpassable for purification, for passing beyond sorrow and despair, for the destruction of suffering and grief.

There are three causes for the arising of karma. Greed is a cause for the arising of karma. Hatred is a cause for the arising of karma. Delusion is a cause for the arising of karma.

It is not non-greed that arises from greed.

It is greed that arises from greed.

It is not non-hatred that arises from hatred.

It is hatred that arises again from hatred.

It is not non-delusion that arises from delusion.

It is delusion that arises from delusion.

The Dharma is directly visible, immediate, inviting one to come and see, worthy of application, to be personally experienced by the wise.

The Venerable Sumana addressed the Buddha:

An arahant, who has lived the spiritual life, has attained the goal. He has no such thought, 'There is none better than I; there is none who is equal; there is none worse.'

The Buddha said: 'It is in such a way that noble ones declare final understanding. So there is no illusion of self.'

'Yet there are some foolish persons who (mistakenly) declare that they have attained such understanding. But afterwards distress befalls them.'

A priest asks: 'What is a householder's aim?'

'Wealth is a householder's aim, his quest is for knowledge, his mainstay is his craft, his desire is for work and his ideal is to bring his work to an end.'

The Buddha: 'Tell me, when in earlier days you lived at home, were you not skilled in playing the lute?'—Sona replied 'Yes.'

'And, when the strings of your lute were too taut, was your lute well tuned and easy to play?'—'No.'

'And when the strings of your lute were too loose, was your lute well tuned and easy to play?'—'No.'

'When the strings of your lute were neither too taut nor too loose, but adjusted to an even pitch, was your lute then well tuned and easy to play?'—'Yes.'

'Similarly, if energy is applied too forcefully it will lead to restlessness, and if energy is too lax it will lead to lassitude. Therefore, keep your energy in balance, penetrate to a balance of these spiritual faculties.'

It is volition that I declare to be karma. Having willed, one produces karma through body, speech or mind.

There are the blessings in realising the fruit of stream-entry (transformation to a noble life):

> One is firm in the Dharma.
>
> One is unable to fall back.
>
> One has set a limit to suffering.
>
> One is endowed with uncommon knowledge.
>
> One has clearly understood causes and the phenomena arising from causes.

A noble student thus endowed will think: No fear do I have for my livelihood. Why should I have fear about it? Have I not the four powers of wisdom, energy, unblemished life and acting benevolently?

It is one who is foolish, lazy, blameworthy and whose conduct in deeds, words and thoughts lacks benevolence who might have fear for his livelihood.

There are eight ways of giving. One gives:

>Spontaneously;
>
>Out of fear;
>
>Because of thinking, 'He too has given me a gift';
>
>Because of thinking, 'He will give me a present, too';
>
>Thinking that it is good to give;
>
>Thinking, 'I cook, but they (being ascetics) do not';
>
>Thinking, 'By giving such a gift, I shall earn a good reputation';
>
>Or one gives because it ennobles the mind.

Virtuous ways of conduct have non-remorse as their benefit and reward.

Non-remorse has gladness as its benefit and reward.

Gladness has joy as its benefit and reward.

Joy has serenity as its benefit and reward.

Serenity has happiness as its benefit and reward.

Happiness has meditative concentration as its benefit and reward.

Meditative concentration has knowing and seeing things as they really are as its benefit and reward.

Knowing and seeing things as they really are has non-attachment as its benefit and reward.

Non-attachment has liberation as its benefit and reward.

In this way, virtuous ways of conduct lead step by step to the highest.

The person of little learning (about the truth of life) grows old like a bull. He grows only in the size of his body but his wisdom does not grow.

What are the blessings of loving-kindness?

If the liberation of the mind by loving-kindness is developed and cultivated, frequently practised, made one's vehicle and foundation, firmly established and properly undertaken, eleven blessings may be expected. What eleven?

> One sleeps peacefully.
>
> One sees no bad dreams.
>
> One is dear to human beings.
>
> One is dear to non-human beings.
>
> One will be protected by angels.
>
> One will feel protected from fire and poison.
>
> One will not feel hurt by weapons.
>
> One's mind becomes easily concentrated in meditation.
>
> One's facial complexion will be serene.
>
> One will die unconfused.
>
> If one does not penetrate higher, one will be reborn in a Divine abiding.

Just as a young man or woman on viewing the image of his or her face in a bright clean mirror would know if there was a spot or no spot, so too, I have proclaimed to my students the way to understand an unliberated mind as unliberated and a liberated mind as liberated.

Ananda to the Buddha: 'Half of the spiritual life is good friendship and good companionship.'

'Not so, Ananda. This is the entire spiritual life, namely good friendship and good companionship.

'When one has a good friend and a good companion, it is to be expected that one will develop and cultivate the Noble Eightfold Path.'

The Kalamas said to the Blessed One:

'There are some ascetics and priests who come to Kesaputta. They explain their own teachings but disparage the teachings of others. For us, there is perplexity and doubt as to who speaks the truth and who speaks falsehood.'

The Buddha said: 'It is fitting for you to be perplexed.'

Do not go by oral tradition,
by lineage,
because it has been widely stated,
by a collection of scriptures,
because it is logical and reasonable,
by inference and drawing conclusions,
because it has been thought out by acceptance of a theory,
by the seeming competence of a speaker,
or because you think, 'This is our teacher'.

But when you know for yourselves, those things censured by the wise which if undertaken and practised lead to harm and suffering, then you should abandon them.

Just as a dewdrop on the tip of a blade of grass will quickly vanish at sunrise and will not last long, so human life is like a dewdrop. It is limited and brief. This one should wisely understand.

Sonadana said:

Gautama, (the Buddha) while youthful, went from the household life into homelessness leaving his parents weeping with tear-stained faces. He is handsome, virtuous, well-spoken, the teacher's teacher of many. He has abandoned sensual desires and dispelled vanity. He teaches action and the way of action, honouring the blameless way of life.

He is a wanderer of high birth. He is a wanderer from a wealthy family. People come to consult him from kingdoms and foreign lands. Many thousands have taken refuge with him.

He is consulted by the chief of the various leaders of sects. Indeed King Seniya Bimbisara of Magadha has gone for refuge to him together with his son, his wife, his followers and his ministers. However much I might praise Gautama, that praise is insufficient, he is beyond all praise.

I declare to you: all conditioned things are of a nature to decay—work out your liberation with diligence. (Last words of the Buddha.)

Outline of the Discourses of the Buddha

⋙══⋘

There are more than 5,500 suttas, or discourses, delivered by the Buddha during his forty-five years of teaching. The suttas are grouped into five *nikayas,* or collections:

THE MIDDLE LENGTH DISCOURSES OF THE BUDDHA translated by Bhikkhu Nanamoli and Bhikkhu Bodhi from *Majjhima Nikaya.* 1,232 pages published in 1995 by Wisdom Publications, 199 Elm Street, Somerville, Boston, MA 02144, USA. Tel: 617 776 7410 ext. 40. Website: www.wisdompubs.org. The 'Middle-length' Discourses (Pali *majjhima* = 'middle') consist of 152 suttas.

THE LONG DISCOURSES OF THE BUDDHA translated by Maurice Walshe from the *Digha Nikaya.* 648 pages published in 1995 by Wisdom Publications, 199 Elm Street, Somerville, Boston, MA 02144, USA. The 'Long' Discourses (Pali *digha* = 'long') consist of 34 suttas.

NUMERICAL DISCOURSES OF THE BUDDHA edited and translated by Bhikkhu Bodhi from the *Anguttara-Nikaya,* published in 2000 by Rowman and Littlefield, USA. Original translation by E.M. Hare from five volumes, approximately 1,400 pages, published in 1978 by Pali Text Society and Unwin Brothers Limited, The Gresham Press, Old Woking, Surrey, England. The discourses consist of 2,308 short suttas, grouped together into eleven *nipatas* according to the number of items of Dharma covered in each sutta. For example, the *Eka-nipata* ('Book of the Ones') contains suttas about a single item of Dharma; the *Duka-nipata* ('Book of the Twos') contains suttas dealing with two items of Dharma, and so on.

THE CONNECTED DISCOURSES OF THE BUDDHA translated by Bhikkhu Bodhi from the *Samyutta-Nikaya.* Approximately 2,000 pages, two volumes, published in November 1995 by Wisdom Publications, 199 Elm Street, Somerville, Boston, MA, 02144, USA. Tel: 617 776 7410 ext. 40. Website: www.wisdompubs.org. This is a collection of thematically-connected short suttas. The discourses consist of 2,889 shorter suttas grouped together into 56 themes.

THE DIVISION OF SHORT BOOKS (Pali *khudda* = 'smaller') consisting of books shorter in length.

THE SUTTA-NIPATA translated by Venerable Saddhatissa. 135 pages, published in 1985 by Curzon Press Limited, 42 Gray's Inn Road, London WC1, England.

THE DHAMMAPADA (423 verses) translated by Venerable Acharya Buddharakkhita with introduction by Bhikkhu Bodhi, published by the Buddhist Publication Society, Kandy, PO Box 61, 54 Sangharaja Mawatha, Kandy, Sri Lanka.

THE UDANA AND THE ITIVUTTAKA translated by John D. Ireland, published by the Buddhist Publication Society, Kandy, PO Box 61, 54 Sangharaja Mawatha, Kandy, Sri Lanka.

MINOR READINGS translated by Bhikkhu Nanamoli, published by the Pali Text Society, 73 Lime Walk, Headington, Oxford OX3 7AD, England.

More than 700 suttas translated by other monks can be found on the website www.accesstoinsight.org.

Glossary

This is a brief definition of various words and terms
used in the context of the quotations.

Arahantship: full knowing of liberation and nothing left to work on in
oneself that can cause suffering.

Attachment: clinging to pleasure, views, rituals and oneself. Freedom
means the end of such attachments, not the end of kindness,
compassion and connection.

Becoming: constantly going on to something different or wanting to
become something different. 'Becoming' refers to what has
become now or what will or might become in the future and the
self's relationship to becoming.

Bodhisattva: a Buddha-to-be, one who lives with deep compassion
and aspires to complete enlightenment.

Bondage: losing oneself in particular situations until one sees a
way out.

Buddha: literally, an Awakened One.

Consciousness: the inner factor of the mind that enables us to be a
conscious human being.

Conditioned: causes and factors that affect any aspect of existence and produce change whether we like it or not.

The Deathless: synonym for Nirvana and a Freedom that death cannot take away.

Delusion: includes confusion, fantasies, fears, getting caught up in self-image etc.

Dependent arising: e.g. a motorcar depends upon numerous parts that are dependently arising together for it to be called a car. 'Dependently arising' applies to everything and everyone.

Desire: wanting for experiences, things, etc., that grip the mind.

Dharma: teachings of the Buddha, the Truth, duty, the nature of things.

Discipline: to follow and apply the Dharma to one's daily life.

Emptiness: the absence of any real inherent substance to phenomena due to dependent arising. Synonym for 'Freedom'. Emptiness implies the Inexpressible and Inconceivable. Emptiness makes everything possible.

Enlightenment: realisation of an indestructible liberation, the emptiness of the ego, a profound opening of the heart, and wise about existence.

Escape from the world: means a wise path or way out of suffering in the world.

Equanimity: the capacity to stay steady in the face of unhealthy patterns and towards pleasurable objects of desire; the capacity to stay steady in the face of painful situations or non-significant situations.

Evil: the deliberate volition to cause great suffering and pain to others.

Faculties: physical and mental features and qualities.

Form: what has shape such as body and material things.

Formations: various states of mind and thoughts that arise due to various patterns and tendencies.

Formless: space, consciousness, etc.

Four great elements: earth, air, heat and liquid.

Gods: evolved spiritual beings.

Gone beyond: not trapped in the world of birth and death and events between the two polarities.

Heaven: a long but temporary period of joy and happiness.

'I' and 'mine': egotism, cherishing of self, self-importance, self-condemnation

I am: in terms of Dharma, indicates a grasping onto a sense of self as if 'I am unique and separate from all else'.

Ignorance: literal translation is 'not knowing'. Not seeing clearly so problems and suffering arise in our life.

Immaterial and limited: e.g., consciousness.

Immaterial and unlimited: e.g., to experience consciousness of oneself is the consciousness of all.

Impurity (in reference to the body): literal translation is 'absence of what is beautiful'.

Karma: unsatisfactory influences from the past that make an impact on the present and generate further volitions and actions in body, speech and mind.

Knowing: indicates a profound knowing in daily life of a true and unshakeable freedom.

Mara: the force of temptation that leads to difficulties.

Material form: includes the physical body and all objects in our surroundings.

Material and limited: e.g., a state of being such as the body.

Material and unlimited: e.g., to experience oneness with everything else.

Meditative Concentration: meditation to ground oneself in the here and now, to see clearly into the nature of things, development of calm, and insight into 'I', 'me' and 'mine'.

Mind Flow: on-going habits and patterns of mind.

Nirvana: liberation from living in greed, hate and delusion. 'Nirvana' is immediately realisable here and now in the midst of life. The ultimate peace that also expresses a fulfilled and awakened life.

No coming and going: indestructible freedom.

Noble Student or Noble One: a transformed person, who knows freedom and lives wisely.

One Thus Gone: an enlightened one. Such a one has gone beyond clinging, wanting, standpoints, egotism and sense of limitation imposed by mind and body.

Practice: three-fold inner development through ethics, meditation and wisdom.

Proliferation: thinking excessively, compelling need to go over issues repeatedly.

Rebirth: the Buddha generally has accepted the doctrine of unresolved forces like waves arising in the ocean of existence. On a couple of occasions, he has adopted a provisional view of belief in rebirth.

Sangha: men and women who have realised a noble transformation.

Tangle: to be caught up in various matters.

Unbecoming, Unborn, Unconditioned, Unmade: synonyms for Liberation or True Freedom that is not made nor dependent on circumstances for its presence. Fulfilment of the spiritual life.

Unconditioned: frequent simile for Liberation or Nirvana. Steady, sublime and unaffected in the midst of things.

Unwholesome: what causes problems for oneself and others through patterns of mind and behaviour.

Wholesome: what brings about benefits for oneself and others.

Useful Addresses

For further information about Buddhist retreat centres,
write to the following organisations.

**MEDITATIONSZENTRUM
BEATENBERG**
Postfach 54
Waldegg
CH Beatenberg
Switzerland
www.karuna.ch

GAIA HOUSE
West Ogwell
Newton Abbot
Devon TQ12 6EN
England
e-mail: gaiahouse@gn.apc.org
www.gn.apc.org/gaiahouse
www.insightmeditation.org

INSIGHT MEDITATION SOCIETY
1230 Pleasant Street
Barre,
MA 01005
USA
www.dharma.org/ims.htm

**SPIRIT ROCK MEDITATION
CENTER**
PO Box 169
Woodacre
CA 94973
USA
e-mail: srmc@spiritrock.org
www.spiritrock.org

Acknowledgements

It was a labour of love to select quotes for *The Buddha's Book of Daily Meditations*. I read the suttas (discourses) and verses of the Buddha contained in around 5,000 pages of translation and explanation of the texts from Pali to English. With so many suttas, it was a fascinating task, and I am full of appreciation for the depth and breadth of the Buddha's understanding of the human experience.

I wish to thank my teachers, Venerable Ajahn Dhammadharo of Supanburi, Thailand, and the late Venerable Ajahn Buddhadassa of Chai Ya, Thailand, both of whom paid respect to the original teachings through their noble lives.

Between 1970–76, I was a Buddhist monk in the Theravada tradition in Thailand. In the early 1970s, Vimalo Kulbarz of Germany patiently guided me through the entire body of suttas (discourses of the Buddha) so that I had a genuine context for my classical training in the Dharma and Insight Meditation (Vipassana). I have endeavoured to pass his precision and enthusiasm for the original teachings on to my students.

I wish to express much gratitude to the eminent scholar-monk, Bhikkhu Bodhi of the Buddhist Publication Society in Sri Lanka, for his careful translation and editing of many thousands of suttas into English. Since the 1970s he has engaged selflessly in this painstaking and detailed task of Buddhist scholarship to make the exact words of the Buddha available in the English language. We are deeply indebted. Bhikkhu Bodhi kindly looked at my selections for this book.

Many thanks also to Guy Armstrong, a Dharma teacher and colleague, who reviewed my selections. Guy also shares a deep love of the suttas.

I wish to thank various publishers, dedicated to the Dharma, for their kind permission to reproduce passages from their books. I have listed their names and addresses on a separate page. I also wish to express gratitude to Anne Ashton, my secretary, for scanning or typing passages that I highlighted. I have spent as much time preparing this book as writing a book of similar length. I enjoyed every minute of it.

I wish to thank my editors, Susan Lascelles and Florence Hamilton of Random House, UK, for their meticulous care.

Many thanks to my mother, late father, Richard Gonski, Dick St. Ruth, Lord Abbots of the Thai Monastery, Bodh Gaya and Sarnath, Gaia House library, Sharpham Buddhist College library; and to the late Thomas Jost from Germany for his many years of dedicated service to Bodh Gaya.

Much gratitude to Nshorna Titmuss, my daughter, for her presence and support.

May all beings live in peace and harmony.

May all beings live wisely.

May all beings be enlightened.

Index

About the Author

CHRISTOPHER TITMUSS is the cofounder of Gaia House, one of the largest and most respected retreat centers in the United Kingdom, and a founding member of the international board of the Buddhist Peace Fellowship. From 1962 to 1967 he worked as a reporter and photojournalist in London, Turkey, Thailand, Laos, and Australia, and then spent six years as a Buddhist monk in Thailand and India. For the last twenty years he has travelled all over the world teaching Awakening and Insight Meditation. He has twice stood for Parliament for the Green Party. He is the author of nine previous books, including *An Awakened Life* and *Light on Enlightenment*.